Victorian
Patchwork & Quilting

Victorian Patchwork & Quilting

Arlene Dettore and Beverly Maxvill

MEREDITH® PRESS

New York, N.Y.

Meredith® Press is an imprint of Meredith® Books:
President, Book Group: Joseph J. Ward
Vice President, Editorial Director: Elizabeth P. Rice

For Meredith Press
Executive Editor: Maryanne Bannon
Senior Editor: Carol Spier
Editor: Ron Harris
Associate Editor: Ruth Weadock
Copy Editor: Susanna Pfeffer
Technical Editor: Ellen Liberles
Production Manager: Bill Rose
Book Design: Remo Cosentino
Photography: Steven Mays
Photo styling: Cathryn Schwing

All of us at Meredith® Press are dedicated to offering you, our customer, the best books we can create. We are particularly concerned that all of our instructions for making projects are clear and accurate. Please address your correspondence to Customer Service, Meredith® Press, 150 East 52nd Street, New York, NY 10022.

If you would like to order additional copies of any of our books, call 1-800-678-8091, or check with your local bookstore.

ISBN: 0-696-20079-1 (hard cover)   ISBN: 0-696-20433-9 (soft cover)
Library of Congress Catalog Card Number: 87-063528

Printed in the United States of America
10 9 8 7 6 5 4 3 2 1

Dear Crafter,

From the very beginning we knew we had something special for our quilters with *Victorian Patchwork & Quilting*. Selecting the projects was a joy, as we sorted through the mountains of stunning quilts, fabulous home decoratives, and wonderful quilted accessories we received from the prolific and expert hands of Beverly Maxvill and Arlene Dettore in St. Clair Shores, Michigan.

Victorian patchwork has always held a place of honor in many quilters' hearts, for both its beauty and its highly personal details: a swatch of favorite fabric here; a pretty bead or bauble there; and embroidered embellishments everywhere. In this book you'll also find the traditional harmonizing with the new as contemporary fabrics and coordinated accent pieces come together with an easy-to-learn piecing technique based on master prints and complementary fabrics.

The eighth annual volume in our series of outstanding quilt books, *Victorian Patchwork & Quilting* is complete with clear, step-by-step directions for each project, accompanied by full-color photographs and helpful illustrations. You'll find projects that are quick and easy and some that are more challenging, for gifts and home accessories for every taste. We hope you'll discover that making them is, as we found creating this book to be, a labor of love.

Enjoy,

Carol Spier

Carol Spier
Senior Editor

How to Use This Book

The first two chapters contain basic craft and sewing information. In "Basic Terms and Techniques" you'll find advice about fabrics, colors, and supplies, plus complete instructions for creating the patchwork. "Embroidery Techniques and Stitches" discusses embroidery threads and equipment, and provides an illustrated glossary of stitches. The remaining chapters are devoted to projects and include color photographs, how-to's, patterns, and illustrations. They consist of "Home Decorations," "Victorian Wearables and Accessories," "Victorian Christmas," "Victorian Baby Gifts," and "Spectacular Quilts." Projects are accompanied by a Color Guide, which describes the fabrics, colors, and embellishments we used. This allows you to duplicate our design as closely as possible if you wish. But we encourage you to let your imagination soar: Choose a different color scheme, use that precious scrap of antique lace you've been saving, try some new embroidery stitches. Do whatever it takes to experience the joy of creating something truly unique!

Arlene Dettore
Arlene Dettore

Beverly C. Maxvill
Beverly Maxvill

Introduction

Needlework rests the mind and organizes the thoughts. Even when one is tired, it is possible to hold patchwork and discover a happiness that brings extra energy and the enthusiasm to do a few stitches. The nineteenth-century English novelist Charles Kingsley must have understood this when he said, "We act as though comfort and luxury were the chief requirements of life, when all we really need to make us happy is something to be enthusiastic about."

The projects in this book take their inspiration from crazy-quilt patchwork, a technique that enjoyed great popularity in the Victorian era. Traditional patchwork requires cutting patches of fabric to exacting measurements and then stitching them together painstakingly to form blocks of intricate geometric designs. The blocks are then assembled to create the quilt top. In crazy-quilt patchwork, however, the shape of the patches is irregular and the patches are sewn together at random. In Victorian days, scraps of silks, satins, velvets, and other luxurious fabrics were used to create the patchwork, which was then lavishly embroidered with fancy stitches.

Because we fell in love with this style of patchwork, we developed our own technique—one that's both simple and elegant. We start with a foundation of thin fleece and then arrange fabric patches, with raw edges turned under, over the entire foundation. (The fleece, by the way, eliminates the need for batting between the quilt top and backing.) We then add embroidery—which keeps the patches in place and holds the edges down—and trims such as lace, eyelet, ribbon, and beads. Whatever the finished project—whether a simple throw pillow or a more challenging quilt—we've found a wonderful creative outlet. We're sure you will too.

Contents

Basic Terms and Techniques

Equipment and Supplies

If you are a home sewer or craftsperson, you probably already own all or most of the following items used for:

Measuring, marking, and cutting: Ruler, yardstick, tape measure; compass; chalk, dressmaker's carbon and tracing wheel, water-soluble marker; dressmaker's shears, scissors, thread snips, rotary cutting wheel, and cutting board.

Making patterns and templates: Tracing paper, heavy paper and/or clear acetate, marking pen or pencil, scissors.

Sewing: Sewing machine, dressmaker's No. 17 silk pins, assorted needles for hand sewing, pincushion, seam ripper, thimble.

Pressing: Steam iron, ironing board, sleeve board, press cloth.

Quilting: Quilting thread and needles (optional), large quilting hoop.

Embroidering: See "Embroidery Techniques and Stitches."

Fabrics and Other Materials

Whether you have a collection of fabrics or need to go on a shopping trip, the following tips will help you "put it all together" for a successful project.

Fabric Prints and Colors

The amounts of fabric listed for each project assume 44- to 45-inch-wide fabrics. If you choose a fabric with a different width, be sure to adjust the amounts accordingly.

When you choose fabrics we suggest you start with a *master print*. The master print is the fabric you fall in love with and with which all the other fabrics will coordinate. Once you have chosen your master print, pick coordinating fabrics that contain the colors in the master print, but do not let them fight or overpower the master print. A combination of a master print (or occasionally, a solid) and 6 or 7 additional fabrics creates a nice flow of color and texture. Here is a guide to help you make your selection.

Master Print + 1 or 2 Solids + 3 or 4 Prints

Master print: Your main print, and usually the largest, this sets the tone for your project. Note that the "master print" may sometimes be a solid.

Solids: These should repeat colors found in the master print. Note that if you choose a chintz fabric (finished with a glaze), you should avoid laying it over another chintz; and it's best to use chintz sparingly.

Prints: Prints may contain two or three colors of the master print, but they should be smaller in scale. You may also choose fabrics that contain only one or two colors of the master print; vary the scale and density of these prints.

A monochromatic (single-color) scheme can be very effective and may be achieved by carefully choosing solids or prints that vary in scale and density. Different sizes as well as reverse prints also offer expanded possibilities.

You will find that your local quilt or specialty fabric stores carry fabric lines that are coordinated in all these ways and that the sales staff are well qualified to help you coordinate several different fabrics. Many of these shops sell "fat quarters"—fabrics that have been split lengthwise down the middle and cut into ½-yard lengths (each piece measures roughly 22 × 18 inches). This size and shape allows maximum flexibility when it comes to preparing strips or patches. Fat quarters are often sold in bundles, either preselected or "mix-and-match."

Fabric Types

Cottons: Fabrics made of 100 percent cotton are easiest to work with. They will hold a crease and thus need fewer pins to keep them in place. Cottons have less resistance to the needle than other fabrics, making it easier to stitch the pieces together. Light colors may shadow (allow darker colors to show through) and may require a lining. Cottons may be torn or cut into strips.

Cotton and polyester blends: The sheer nature of many blends requires that they be lined. These fabrics also tend to be a little slippery and need more pinning to hold them in place. Cut all strips.

Velvets and brocades: The weight and bulk of these fabrics make them harder to sew through, so it's best not to turn under any edges. Place the fabric in the desired spot and turn under the seam allowance of the adjacent fabrics. If you place two pieces of velvet together, you should butt the edges rather than overlapping them. Choose a ribbon to cover the adjoining edges and stitch in place. Cut all strips.

Novelty and other unusual fabrics: When temptation strikes, do not throw caution to the winds. While you may be attracted to a special fabric, you should consider how difficult it may be to handle and sew and how it can be cleaned. We have used napkins, linens, sheets, old clothing, handkerchiefs, and decorator fabrics. If you are considering using something similar and feel it can work with your other fabrics, by all means use it!

Embellishments

Adding embroidery (see "Embroidery Techniques and Stitches," pages 30–39) and other embellishments serves two purposes: (1) to hold down all those folded edges that are part of your layout and (2) to add a decorative, personal, and creative touch to your project.

Lace: All lace trims should be laundered and preshrunk before you place them on your layout. Pregathered lace edgings should be cut away from the bound or gathered edge so they will lie flat. Unfinished edges should be covered by a turned-under edge of fabric. Finished edges are usually positioned ⅛ inch in from the folded edge of a fabric strip.

Antique linens: You can use portions (including edgings and appliqués) of old handkerchiefs, pillowcases, and table linens. This is a great way of recycling pieces that are worn, and they add an antique look to your work. Before using them, however, you should remove any stains and preshrink if necessary.

Eyelet: You can use pregathered eyelet trim as is, or if you want them to lie flat, you can cut them away from any binding (see "Lace," earlier). If you use an eyelet fabric as part of your project layout, you will need a lining of the same color—or try a contrasting color to show off the design.

Ribbons: A wonderful variety of ribbons is available in all fabrics and widths. Be sure to preshrink all ribbons before use.

Buttons: Old, new, and novelty buttons make great embellishments for your project.

Beads and other ornaments: You can add seed, bugle, and an ever-expanding variety of beads to your projects. It's best to add beads after your project is assembled, since they can catch your threads as you work and slow you down. Omit beads or similar embellishments on toys or other projects intended for small children.

Foundation or Base Fabrics

Pellon® fleece: This polyester fabric is a very thin, firm batting. It is 45 inches wide and is available by the yard. Pellon fleece is easy to stitch and adds a slightly puffy look to your work. If a larger piece is needed, join by butting edges together; then zigzag-stitch by machine or whipstitch by hand. You can use Pellon fleece for most of the projects in this book—pillows, quilts, table runners, and so on.

Cotton-and-polyester batting: Several companies make a cotton-and-polyester-blend batting that can be used in place of the Pellon fleece just discussed.

Muslin: For clothing projects we recommend 100 percent cotton muslin, which makes a very lightweight foundation. Preshrink, then cut into the required shape.

Threads

For sewing and assembling your projects, you may use any all-purpose sewing thread. Any all-cotton, all-polyester, or cotton-wrapped polyester thread, in a color that blends with your master print, would be a good choice. Use the same type of thread for machine quilting. For hand quilting, you may wish to try a special quilting thread. For a description of embroidery threads, see "Embroidery Techniques and Stitches."

Care and Laundering

When choosing fabrics and embellishments for your projects note the recommended laundering instructions, and be sure to choose materials that require similar care. In other words, if you wash and dry *one,* then you must wash and dry *all.* Preshrink all washable fabrics, trims, lace, ribbons, and appliqués before use.

Your (washable) finished projects may be laundered with a mild soap or detergent. Turn sweatshirts inside out; place small items, such as pillows or table runners, in a pillowcase or mesh bag. If the item is too large for a bag, baste it closed with the decorative stitching to the inside.

Machine-wash using the delicate cycle, and spin out excess water. Then lay your piece out flat to dry. If it is very large you can dry it in the dryer (in bag or basted closed) for 5 to 10 minutes, but be sure to remove it immediately; lay it flat to finish drying. Never attempt to dry your piece completely in the dryer. Thread, especially the all-cotton variety, tends to shrink, causing puckers.

If your finished project must be dry-cleaned, try to save a small sample of each fabric and trim for testing before cleaning the entire piece.

Layout and Embellishment Techniques

Preparing Fabrics for Layout

You will need to tear or cut your fabrics into strips to create the layout. For larger projects, such as quilts, table covers, and wall hangings, strips may vary in width from 3½ to 6½ inches and are usually at least 18 inches long. For smaller projects, strips may be narrower and shorter. All strips must be on the *straight grain* (parallel to the selvage edge), as shown (Figure 1). You may cut with shears or a rotary cutter.

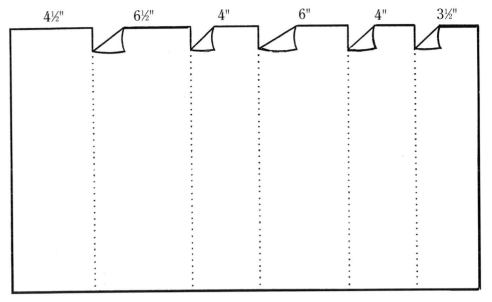

4½"   6½"   4"   6"   4"   3½"

Cut 18" or longer

Figure 1

Creating the Layout

Here are the basic techniques needed to lay out your pieces. We suggest that you take some time to practice the folding and pinning, to familiarize yourself with the technique. Also note the two-letter abbreviations that are used in the layout diagrams.

First piece: Your very first strip will have no folds. Simply place in the position shown in the layout diagram and pin in place, as shown (Figure 2).

Single fold (SF): Once you have torn or cut all of your strips, as you pick up each one, turn the top edge (long edge) under ½ inch, as shown (Figure 3). Once you have positioned this strip on the layout, place pins along the folded edge only (Figure 4).

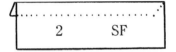

Figure 3

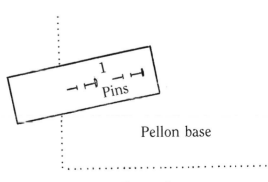

Figure 2

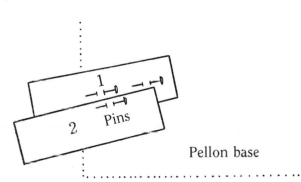

Figure 4

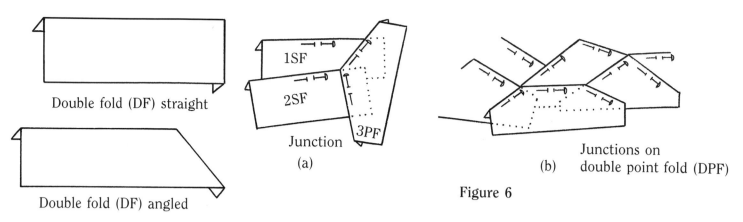

Double fold (DF) straight

Double fold (DF) angled

Figure 5

Junction
(a)

1SF

2SF

3PF

Junctions on
(b) double point fold (DPF)

Figure 6

Double fold (DF): The first fold is along the top edge (SF) and the second is at the right edge; this second fold may be straight or angled (Figure 5). Place pins along both folded edges.

Point fold (PF): The point fold helps to shape and control the layout. After placing 2 or more strips in parallel positions, you will create a point fold to add shaping and flow to the layout. Shown is a single fold across another single fold, with a point fold at the junction (Figure 6a), and a double point fold (DPF) (Figure 6b). To pivot, turn under more than ½ inch, as needed, to create the desired angle, placing the pin at the point before you pivot. Note that the dotted line represents the fabrics underneath the new strip.

Interlock (IL): Wherever a double fold is placed on top of another, you should interlock the folded edges for a smooth and even edge.

Example A: Lay a SF strip across the DF strip that is already in place, maintaining a ½-inch overlap across the bottom (raw) edge; then pin in place (Figure 7a). At the end of the strip, as you turn under the end, lift the double fold and wrap the top strip over the bottom strip, creating an interlock; pin (Figure 7b).

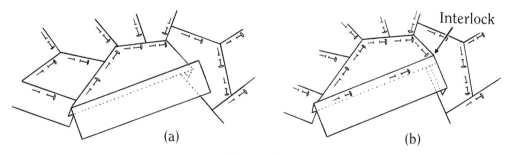

Interlock

(a)

(b)

Figure 7

Example B: This type of interlock is used at the neck edge of sweatshirts or wherever you need to end your layout at a marked edge, rather than at the edge of the foundation you are working on. The first piece interlocks at the neck edge only. The second piece interlocks at the right edge and then interlocks at the marked edge and creates a finished edge. Pin both folds in place (Figure 8).

Pinning: We recommend using No. 17 silk pins, which are fine and sharp and will slip easily through all layers. The pins should be placed along the folded edge(s) of your strip. You will need more than 120 pins for an average project.

Trimming excess fabric: As you place each strip in position and pin it down, trim the excess. Do not fold edges to be covered by pieces yet to be added. Always cut straight across the strip (Figure 9), with the grain, rather than trying to shape it by cutting on an angle. The layout diagrams will show how the fabrics are layered under the new strips. Once your new strip is in place you may lift and trim excess fabric.

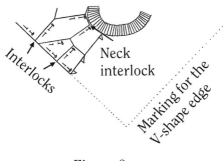

Figure 8

Basic Layout: 14- to 18-inch Square

Cut base fabric to desired size. Starting at center of left-hand edge as shown (Figure 10), place #1 at angle and pin in place. Then:

    #2: SF across #1, pin.
    #3: SF across #2, pin.
    #4: PF across #3 and #2, pin.
    #5: SF across #4, pin.

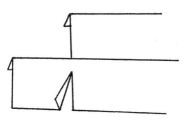

Figure 9

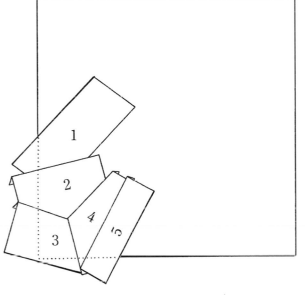

Figure 10

As you add strips to the layout, always work from left to right and from top to bottom, covering the base fabric completely as you go. Trim excess fabric even with the base, then turn the square 90 degrees clockwise and continue the layout as shown (Figure 11).

  #6: DF across #5, #4, and #2, straight end at #1, pin.
  #7: DF across #6, IL with #6, pin.
  #8: PF across #5 and #6, pin.
  #9: SF across #8, #6, and #7, pin.
  #10: SF across #9, pin.
  #11: SF across #10, pin.

Trim and turn as before; then continue the layout as shown (Figure 12).

  #12: PF across #9 and #7, pin.
  #13: DF across #11, #10, and #12, pin.
  #14: PF across #13 and #12, pin.
  #15: DPF across #14, #12, and #7, pin.
  #16: SF across #14, pin.
  #17: PF across #16 and #15, pin.
  #18: SF across #16 and #17, pin.
  #19: SF across #18, pin.

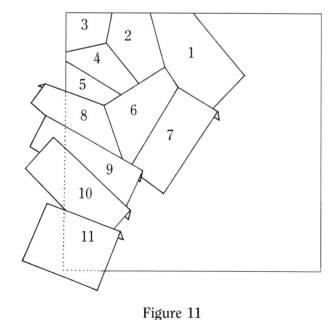

Figure 11

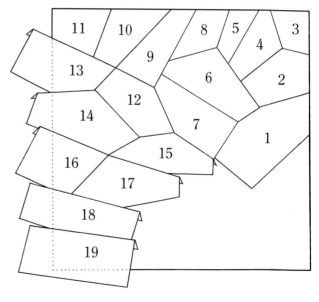

Figure 12

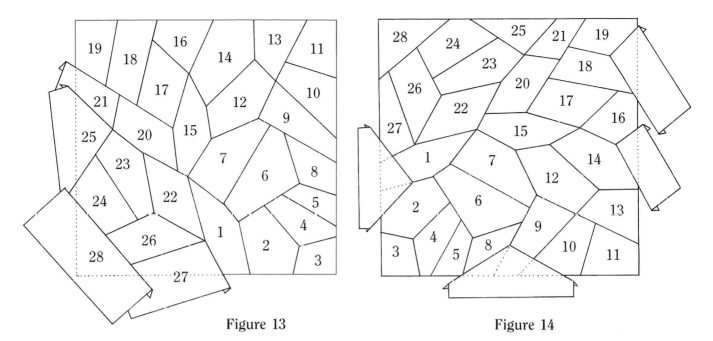

Figure 13   Figure 14

Trim and turn as before, then continue the layout as shown (Figure 13).

    #20: PF across #18, #17, and #15, pin.
    #21: DF across #19, #18, and #20, pin.
    #22: PF across #20, #15, and #1, pin.
    #23: PF across #20 and #22, pin.
    #24: SF across #23, pin.
    #25: PF across #21, #23, and #24, pin.
    #26: PF across #24, #23, and #22, pin.
    #27: DF across #26 and #1, pin.
    #28: SF across #24, #26, and #27, pin.

Trim remaining excess fabric.

Finishing: When you have finished your layout turn it back to the starting position and look it over. If any edges have an area with a strip-pieced look, you can correct it with a double-fold or point-fold strip (Figure 14). You can also use this method if you feel the colors aren't distributed evenly. Simply add a strip or strips of the required print or color.

If you are adding laces or other trim, you should apply them to the layout at this time (see page 24). You are now ready to embroider your piece (see "Embroidery Techniques and Stitches").*

*The layouts provided in this book are to be used as a guide and need not be followed exactly. As you learn to manipulate the strips of fabric, you will devise your own layouts, and the number needed to cover an area will vary.

Intermediate Layout: 20- to 28-inch Square

Cut base fabric to desired size. Mark the center of each edge; then join marks to divide square into quarters. Now, starting at center of left-hand side with #1, begin adding strips as shown (Figure 15). Remember to work from left to right and from top to bottom, turning your foundation—and layout diagram—clockwise as you complete each quarter.

First quarter is #1 through #15; second quarter is #16 through #30; third quarter is #31 through #46; and fourth quarter is #47 through #58. When all four quarters have been completed, turn piece wrong side up and trim excess fabric even with foundation edges. Add trims and embroidery as for Basic Layout, earlier.

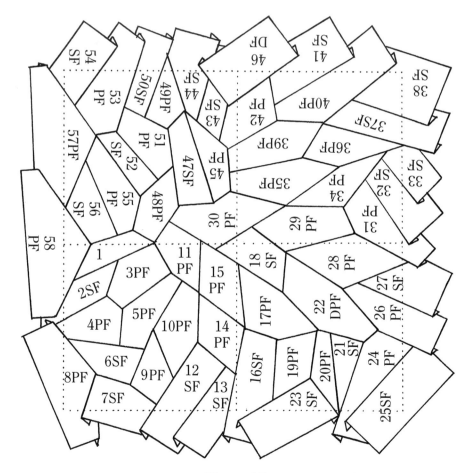

Figure 15

Advanced Layout: 44-inch Square or Circle

This layout is given as an alternative to the basic square layout. It is worked in a somewhat circular fashion, starting at the center of the top edge. You do not need to follow it exactly, but it is a good method for using the double-point or double-fold technique to get out of a tight corner. This layout makes heavy use of interlocking on many edges, especially when double folds are used along a straight edge—for example, 9 (DF) to 10 (DF) to 11 (PF) (Figure 16).

If you prefer, you may use this layout by dividing the base fabric into quarters (see Intermediate Layout, earlier) and starting at the center of the left-hand edge.

Circular Layout

To create a circular layout, cut the base fabric into a circle before you begin adding strips; instructions for cutting a circle follow. The dotted line on the layout (Figure 16) represents the circle; whenever the number sequence falls outside the circle simply skip to the next number within the circle.

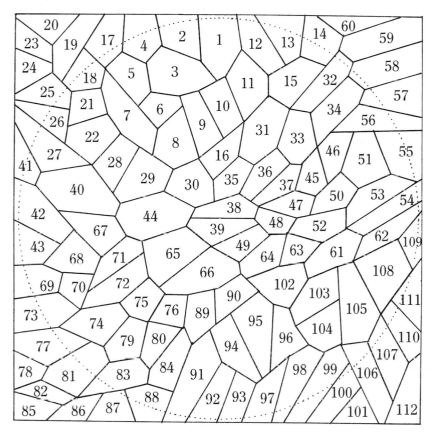

Figure 16

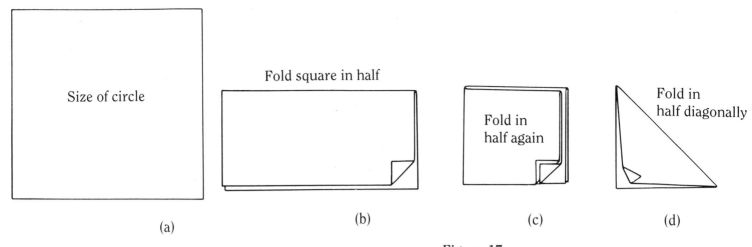

Size of circle

Fold square in half

Fold in half again

Fold in half diagonally

(a)

(b)

(c)

(d)

Figure 17

Cutting a circle: Cut a square of base fabric the desired size of your circle (Figure 17a). Fold square in half horizontally (Figure 17b), then in half again vertically (Figure 17c). Now fold this smaller square in half diagonally (Figure 17d). Tie a marking pen to a length of string; fasten the other end of the string to the point of the folded fabric, then mark the circle as shown (Figure 18). Trim fabric along marked line, then unfold.

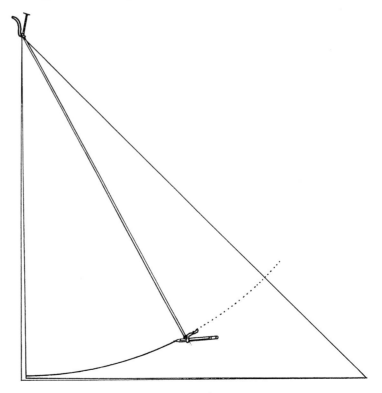

Figure 18

Layouts for Individual Projects

Follow the preceding techniques as you follow the layout patterns for your project, adding each patchwork piece in numerical order, folding as needed to cover the edges of previously pinned pieces as shown.

Special Layout Techniques: Fan

Using a straight or angled double fold, shape a fan in a corner or in any desired position, as shown (Figure 19).

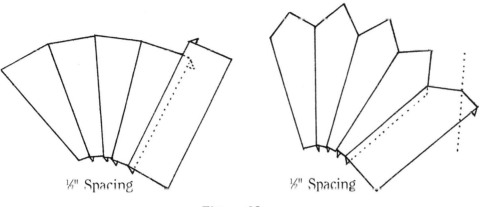

⅛" Spacing   ⅛" Spacing

Figure 19

Reducing bulk: As you pin strips in place, lift and trim excess, leaving a ½-inch seam allowance. The bottom of the fan will be the most difficult area, so choose one of the following treatments (Figure 20), then trim excess fabric.

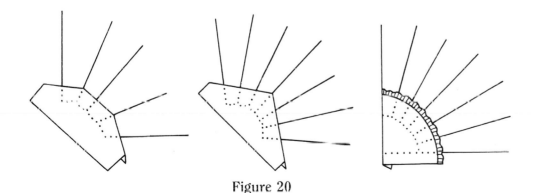

Figure 20

Special Embellishment Techniques

Trims with unfinished edges: If your lace or trim has one unfinished edge, slip it ½ inch under a folded edge of fabric, pin in place, and sew along the fold. Then, if the trim is wide and you do not want the finished edge to remain free, hold it down with French knots or another embroidery stitch (Figure 21).

Trims with finished edges: Place over the folded edge of fabric; then, using a running or chain stitch, anchor the trim and fabric to the base (Figure 22). Slip the ends under an adjacent fabric, or, leaving a ½-inch seam allowance, trim and fold over the edge of the base fabric (Figure 22). Both edges of trim may be embroidered, as shown (Figure 22).

Appliqués, doilies, and handkerchiefs: All of these items can be added, using the preceding techniques. It is not always necessary to remove trims on these items from their base fabrics; simply cut and apply as described earlier, then embroider near the edges to keep them flat (Figure 23).

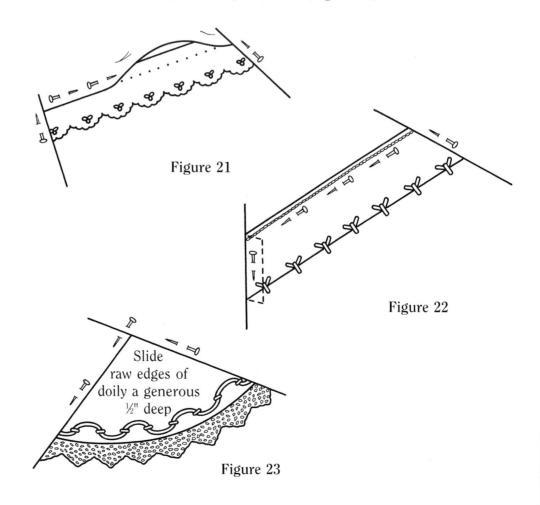

Figure 21

Figure 22

Slide raw edges of doily a generous ½" deep

Figure 23

24

Additional Craft and Sewing Techniques

Following are some other techniques that you may find useful as you create the projects in this book.

Enlarging Patterns

Have patterns enlarged on a professional copy machine, or transpose them by hand to a full-size grid drawn on graph paper (see individual project instructions for size of grid squares) as follows:

First, mark the same number of rows and columns of grid squares on graph paper as on the original grid, as shown (Figures 24a, b). Then, on the full-size grid, mark where the pattern lines intersect the grid lines, and connect the markings, as shown (Figures 24c, d).

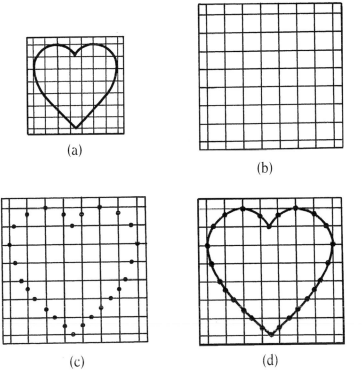

(a)

(b)

(c)   (d)

Figure 24

Transferring Designs

If your fabric is lightweight and light-colored, place it over the design to be copied and, using a chalk pencil or other fabric marker, trace the design directly onto the fabric. (To enhance visibility, you can go over the design to be transferred with a fine marking pen.)

To transfer a design that is not visible through the fabric, use dressmaker's carbon in a color that will be visible on your fabric without great contrast. Place the design to be transferred in position on your fabric; then place the carbon colored side down between the design and the fabric and, with a tracing wheel, stylus, or pencil, go over all design lines to transfer them to the fabric.

Cutting Sashing Strips, Borders, and Binding

The directions give exact measurements for the length of sashing strips, borders, and binding strips needed for finishing your quilt. However, to allow for the individual variations that can occur in any handcrafted project, you may want to cut these strips a little longer than suggested and then to trim off any excess as you join them to your completed quilt. Or you can mark off strips on fabric as directed, but do not cut them until you are ready to use them; then add any needed adjustments.

Joining Ends of Welting or Corded Piping

When cutting welting to fit the project, add 1 inch to the needed length. Once the welting is pinned in place, begin stitching 1 inch away from the starting end of the welting, and stop 1 inch before reaching the other end. At ends, open the welting and trim the ends of the filler cord so they just meet, as shown (Figure 25a). Turn one end of the fabric covering under ½ inch and lap the other end over it (Figure 25a). Then reposition the fabric over the cord and finish stitching, as shown (Figure 25b).

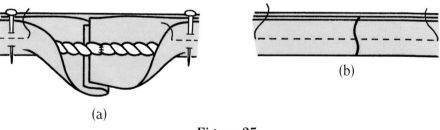

(a)

(b)

Figure 25

Joining Ends of Binding

Cut binding 1 inch longer than needed length. Turn the starting end under ½ inch, then pin binding in place. At the other end turn excess binding under ½ inch or as needed so the turned ends just meet. Continue to apply binding as your project instructions direct.

Mitering Corners of Binding

Stitch prepared binding in place along edge, stopping ¼ inch before you reach the corner, as shown (Figure 26a). Backstitch to lock in place. Raise the press-

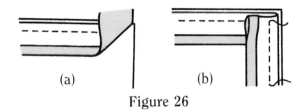

(a)   (b)

Figure 26

er foot and cut the thread. Fold the binding diagonally to turn the corner, as shown (Figure 26a). Lower the needle into the fabric ¼ inch from the corner, pivot the fabric, and resume stitching, as shown (Figure 26b). When slip-stitching the opposite edge of the binding in place, form another diagonal fold at each corner to complete the miter.

Making a Rod Pocket

Cut leftover backing fabric 3½ inches wide and 1 inch shorter than the finished width of the quilt or wall hanging. Press the long edges under ¼ inch. Press the short ends under ¼ inch twice, then stitch these short hems in place. Prepare the quilt backing, piecing if necessary. Before assembling the quilt top and backing, pin the pressed strip to the right side of the backing about 1 inch from the top edge and centering the ends between the side edges. Leaving the hemmed ends open, stitch the strip in place along the long edges, forming a pocket for a rod. Assemble and complete the quilt as directed in the project instructions.

Note: If the border is going to be quilted, the rod pocket is sewn on by hand after the quilt is completed.

Marking Scallops

The scallop templates allow you to mark the cutaway section between the scallops. Trace the template, placing the dotted side edge on the fold of paper; cut the shape and open it out for a complete template. Mark the quilt edge for the indicated number of evenly spaced scallops (or begin at the center and mark toward the corners). Use the template to draw the notch and curve of the scallops, adjusting as needed at the center of the scallop (narrow edge of the template) to make evenly rounded scallops across; mark a gracefully curved scallop at each corner.

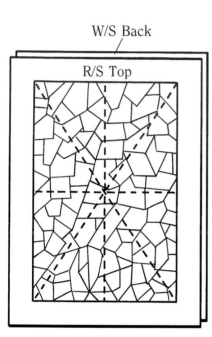

W/S Back

R/S Top

Figure 27

Quilting Techniques

Piecing the Backing

If your quilt is wider than 45 inches, you will need to piece the backing. For quilts up to 88 inches wide, you will need twice the *length* of the quilt for the backing, plus a few extra inches. For example, if your quilt is 72 inches long, you will need 144 inches, or 4 yards (plus a few extra inches) for the backing. Cut the backing fabric crosswise into 2 equal pieces. Sew panels together the long way.

Assembling the Quilt Layers

Traditionally, quilts have three layers: the top, the batting, and the backing. Since the quilts in this book are made with Pellon fleece as the foundation for the patchwork top, they don't require a middle layer, because the fleece takes the place of the batting. To assemble the quilt, place the backing *wrong* side up on a flat surface; then place the patchwork top right side up over the backing, lining up the edges. Pin the layers together all around. Then, using a needle and contrasting thread, baste the layers together as shown (Figure 27), always beginning in the center and working outward. Baste around the edges last, unless your project instructions say otherwise. (Safety pin basting is acceptable.)

Quilting

Quilting—stitching the layers together along seamlines or in a decorative design—is optional; your project instructions will tell you whether it is called for, and whether to quilt by hand or by machine. Once you have completed the quilting, remove the basting. Finish the edges of the quilt as directed, usually by binding.

Making Bias Binding

Packaged, prefolded bias tape in narrow and wide widths is available in a variety of colors. If you prefer to make your own binding, you can do so as follows: First decide on the finished width of the binding; multiply by 2, then add ½ inch to get the cut width. For example, to make a binding with a finished width of ½ inch, cut the binding strip 1¼ inches wide.

Before cutting the strips, straighten the crosswise edge of the fabric by tearing across or by pulling a crosswise thread and cutting along it. Then fold the fabric diagonally so the selvage edge matches the crosswise edge; this is the true bias. Press the fold, then open the fabric and, using pencil and yardstick, mark lines parallel to the crease equal in width to the figure you determined earlier.

To join the bias strips in one continuous step, number the marked strips and cut away the excess as shown (Figure 28). Then, with right sides together, pin the numbered edges together to form a tube, pinning one end of strip 1 to the opposite end of strip 2, and so on, as shown (Figure 29). Note that first and last strips are offset. Stitch, taking a ¼-inch seam. Press the seam allowances open; then, beginning at the free end of strip 1, cut in a spiral along the marked lines, as shown (Figure 29). Make enough bias strips in this way to fit around the edge to be bound, plus a few extra inches.

To prepare the joined bias strip for binding, press both long edges under ¼ inch; then fold the strip in half lengthwise with wrong sides together and press.

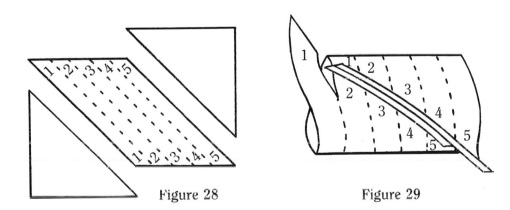

Figure 28   Figure 29

Embroidery Techniques and Stitches

Embroidery Materials and Equipment

Threads

An infinite variety of embroidery threads is available; we mention just a few of our favorites here.

Pearl cotton: A twisted thread with a slight sheen, pearl cotton comes in three weights: No. 8 is the thinnest and lightest, No. 3 is the heaviest and thickest, and No. 5 is in between. No. 8 pearl cotton is the most commonly used size for embroidering the designs in this book, and if the size is not specified, it is the one you should use. It is available in many colors, in both solids and variegated shades. You should use at least 3 to 4 colors per project, and preferably more, especially for large or complicated projects. You will find it comfortable to work with 18- to 24-inch lengths of thread.

The heavier No. 3 and No. 5 threads are ideal for creating a more distinct or textured effect, or for making tassels or twisted cord.

Rayon: Similar in texture to pearl cotton, but with a more pronounced sheen. Use it for embellishing or highlighting stitches rather than for holding fabrics to their foundation. Since rayon threads are not as strong as cotton, you should use shorter lengths of 12 to 15 inches.

Metallics and other novelty threads: Use these sparingly in combination with pearl cotton to create weaving and other special effects. Metallics are especially effective on Christmas projects.

Note: No matter what thread you are using, whenever you have a tail end (4 to 6 inches) left in your needle, keep it in the needle rather than discarding it. This tail end will often be enough for a French knot or other small stitch—either alone or in a group—to finish off a design!

Supplies

"Basic Terms and Techniques" lists and describes the equipment and supplies needed by home sewers and crafters. In addition, you will need the following:

Box. Choose a covered plastic box with compartments of different sizes to store balls of thread and other supplies. If you are working on more than one project at a time, keep a separate box for each project, containing all the colors and supplies you need for each. This way you won't have to raid another project's box for a needed item.

Magnetic tape. Put a strip of magnetic tape inside the lid, to hold threaded needles.

Crochet hook. This is handy for pulling short thread ends to the back; it also aids in making knots.

Small pliers, needle grabbers, index cards/pencil (for jotting down notes), and adhesive bandages will also be useful.

Embellishing the Layout with Embroidery

The stitch diagrams on pages 34–39 illustrate how to work a number of embroidery stitches. The basic stitch is shown first, followed by several variations. Try some new ones!

The first illustration (Figure 1) shows how embroidery stitches are used to secure the patches to the Pellon fleece foundation, while adding embellishment at the same time. Begin stitching at the outer edge of the layout, using the basic form of the stitches you have chosen. Place the stitches along only the folded edges of the patches, removing pins as you go. As you finish stitching one patch you can easily begin a different stitch along the edge of a new fabric patch. The second illustration (Figure 2) shows how to embellish the original lines of stitching and add new stitches.

Also see page 24 for how to handle special embellishments (trims, appliqués, doilies, etc.).

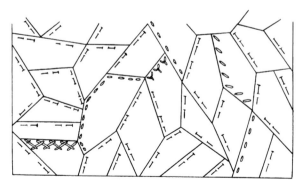

Figure 1

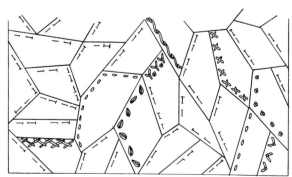

Figure 2

Tassels

Using No. 8 pearl cotton in your needle, wrap the thread around your finger 20 times (Figure 3a). Slip threaded end of needle back under wraps, leaving a loop (Figure 3b). Insert needle back through loop (Figure 3c). Pull tight to close loop; then slip the wraps off your finger.

Keeping needle threaded, hold wraps near bottom and insert point of needle ¼ inch from top (Figure 3d). Wind thread tightly 3 times ¼ inch from top; then insert point of needle under wound threads and through the very top (Figure 3e). Cut loops at bottom of tassel and trim ends so they are even.

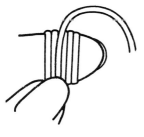

(a)

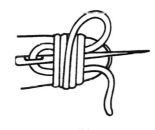

(b)

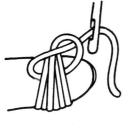

(c)

(d)

(e)

Figure 3

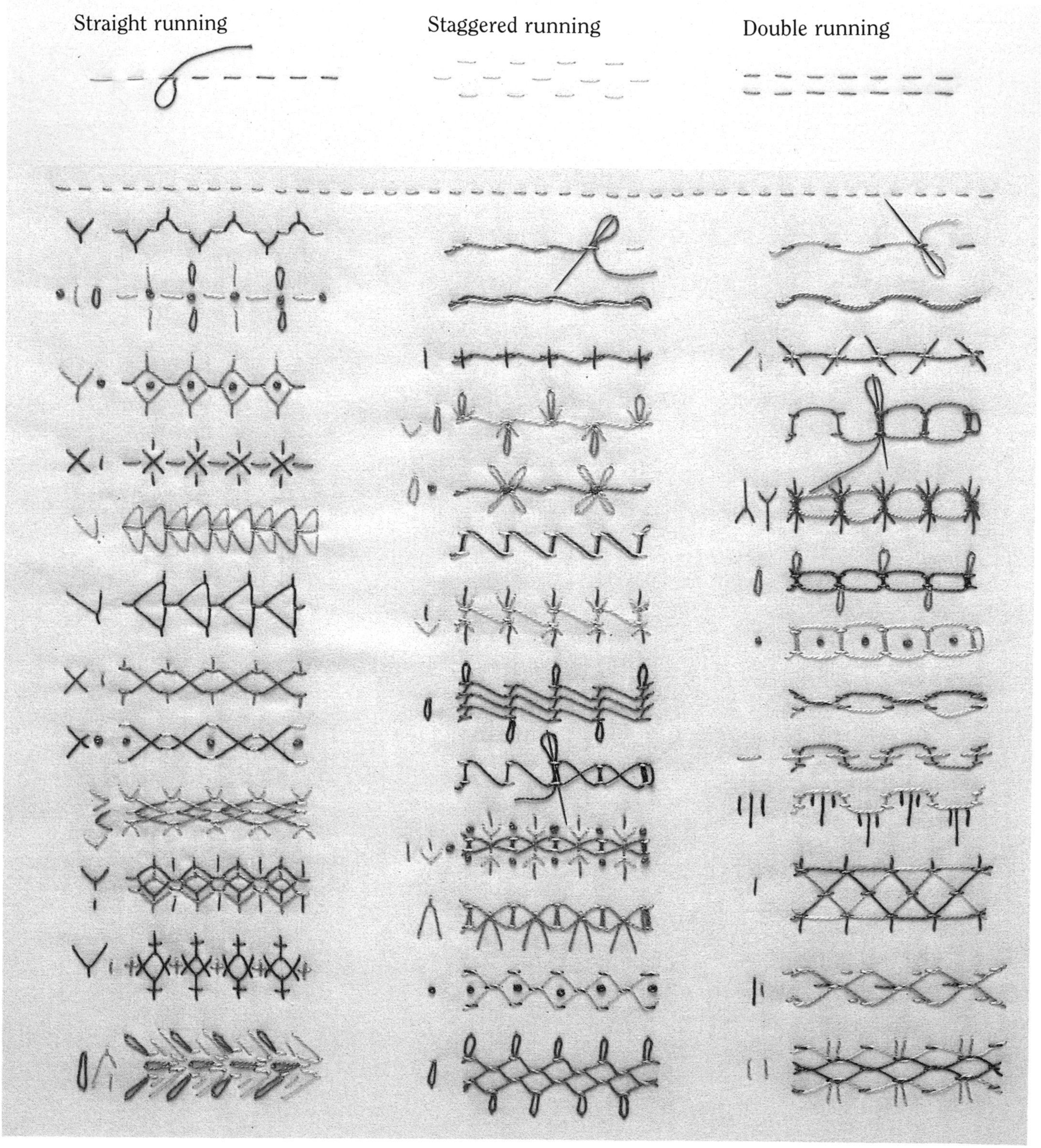
Straight running
Staggered running
Double running

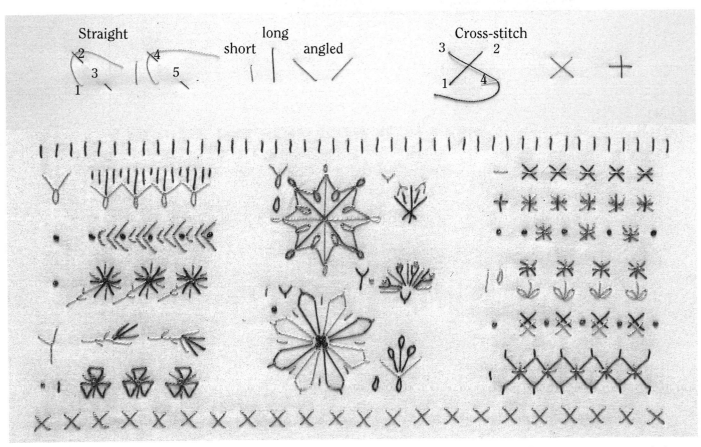

Straight

2 4
3 5
1

long
short angled

Cross-stitch

3 2
1 4

✕ ＋

Stitch Diagrams: The basic stitch is shown first, followed by several variations of the basic stitch. When the basic stitch is combined with other stitches, the symbols for the additional stitches are given to the left of each stitch pattern (see the key to symbols below). Some patterns use 2 or more colors of thread.

Use these patterns as a guide; then create your own variations and combinations.

Stitch Glossary: The symbol in front of the stitch name is the simplest form of the stitch. Other variations are shown at the top of the stitch page next to the how-to illustrations.

SYMBOL	STITCH NAME	PAGE	SYMBOL	STITCH NAME	PAGE	SYMBOL	STITCH NAME	PAGE
- - -	Running	34	⌒⌒	Chain	37	〜〜	Cretan–Herringbone (mixed)	36
⌒	Whipped running	34	0 0	Detached chain (Lazy-daisy)	37	‖‖‖	Straight	35
⌒	Threaded running	34	Y	Fly–Chain anchor	37	＋	Cross-stitch	35
⊔⊔⊔	Buttonhole	38	⟩⟩⟩	Feather	38	•	French knot	39
Y	Fly	39	⋉⋊	Herringbone	36	—	Bullion	39
∆	Slanted buttonhole	38	〜〜	Cretan	36			

35

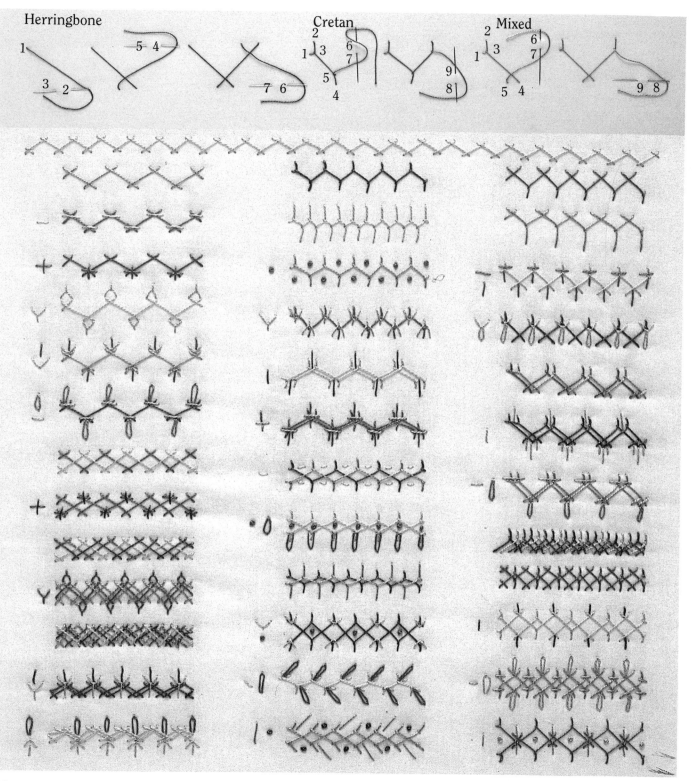

Herringbone

1
3 2
5 4
7 6

Cretan

2
1 3
6
7
5
4
9
8

Mixed

2
1 3
6
7
5 4
9 8

36

Chain

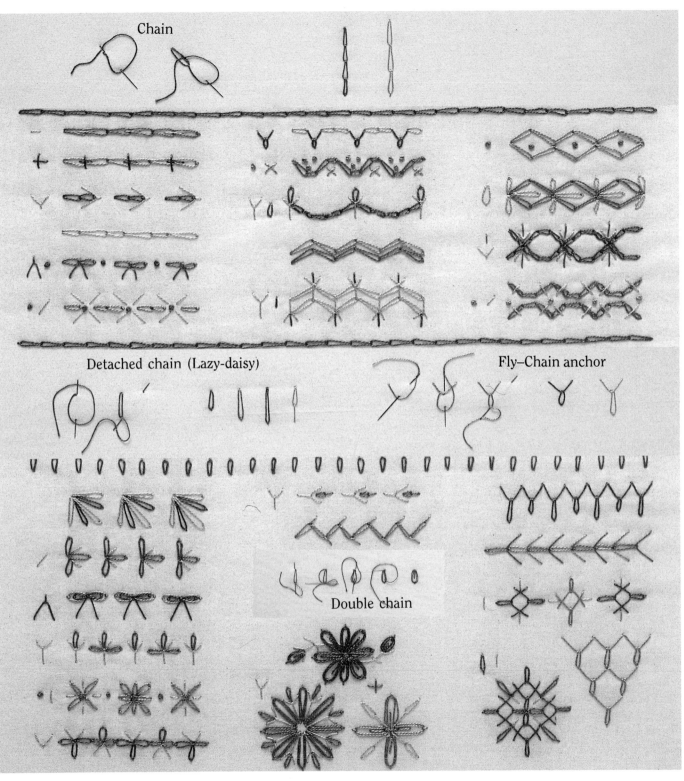

Detached chain (Lazy-daisy)

Fly–Chain anchor

Double chain

Buttonhole

Slanted buttonhole

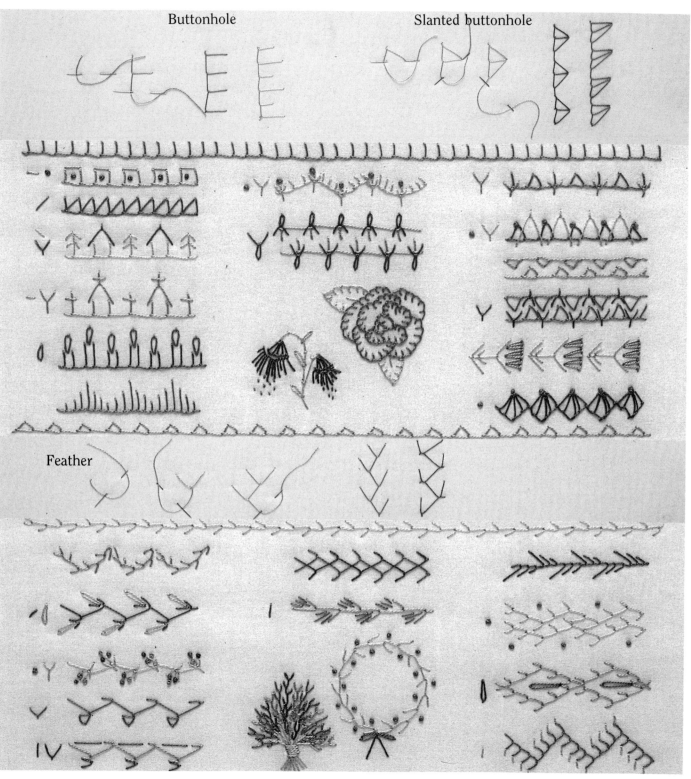

Feather

Fly

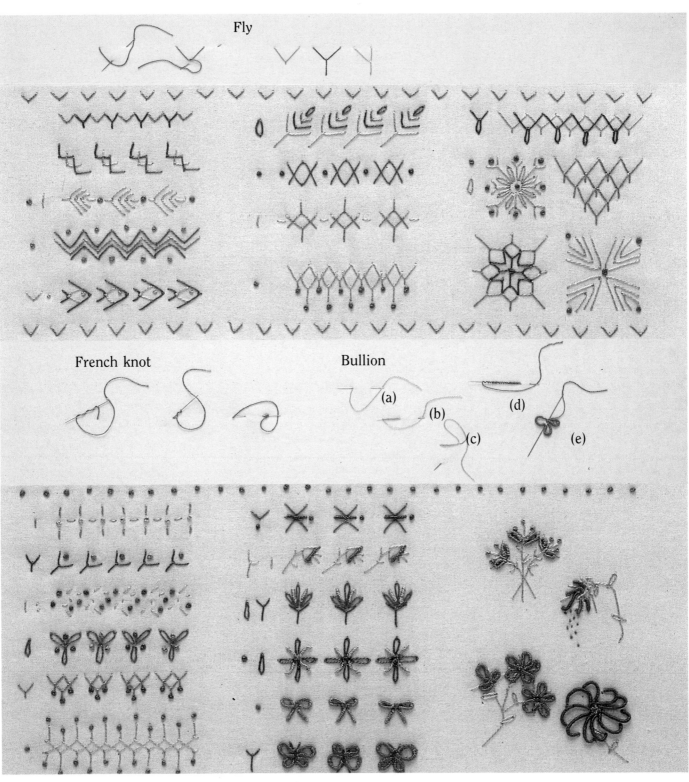

French knot

Bullion

(a)

(b)

(c)

(d)

(e)

39

Home Decorations

Pastel Pillows

Sizes: Ruffled square (center), 14 × 14 inches; ruffled rectangle (back), 12 × 16 inches; crochet-edged heart (front), 14 inches across; all sizes exclude ruffle/edging.

Note: Instructions for the Victorian Vest are on page 73.

Materials (enough for 2 pillows, any size)

Note: All fabrics are 45 inches wide.
½ yard master print
¼ yard each of 5 to 7 coordinating fabrics, including 1 or 2 solids
½ yard Pellon fleece
Assorted lace appliqués and trims (see "Basic Terms and Techniques")
Embroidery materials (see "Embroidery Techniques and Stitches")
½ yard backing fabric

For each square pillow: 1¾ yards pregathered ruffling, 2 inches wide
14-inch-square pillow form or polyester stuffing

For each rectangular pillow: 1¾ yards each of pregathered eyelet edging,
  1¼ inches wide, and flat, Cluny-type lace, ¾ inch wide
Polyester stuffing

For each heart pillow: 2½ yards crocheted edging, about 1¼ inches wide
Polyester stuffing
Paper for pattern

Directions

Note: All measurements include ¼-inch seam allowances.

Square Pillow

Patchwork layout: For each pillow, cut a 14½-inch square of Pellon fleece for the layout foundation. Follow the instructions for Basic Layout (pages 17–19) to create a patchwork piece for the pillow top. Then, using trims and embroidery stitches, embellish the entire layout as desired (see "Basic Terms and Techniques" and "Embroidery Techniques and Stitches").

Ruffle: Cut pregathered ruffling to fit around the patchwork square plus 1 inch. Join ends, making a French seam as follows: With *wrong* sides together, stitch ends together ⅛ inch from edge to form a ring. Then, with right sides together and enclosing previously stitched seam, stitch ends together again, taking a ¼-inch seam (Figure 1). Press this French seam to one side. With

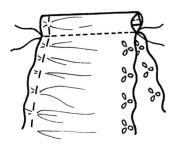

Figure 1

right sides together and ruffle facing center of pillow top, pin bound (or unfinished) edge of ruffle to patchwork pillow top, placing French seam at center of one side of square, and easing ruffle around corners as shown (Figure 2). Machine-baste all around.

Finishing: From backing fabric cut a square the same size as patchwork pillow top. With right sides together and edges matching, pin top and backing together, enclosing ruffle. Stitch around 4 corners and 3 sides, leaving an opening for turning and stuffing. Grade seam allowances, trim corners, and turn right side out. Insert pillow form or stuff with polyester stuffing. Turn opening edges under and slipstitch opening closed.

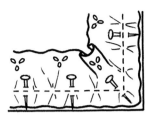

Figure 2

Rectangular Pillow

Patchwork layout: Follow directions for Square Pillow, above, *except* cut Pellon fleece foundation 16½ × 12½ inches. Embellish with lace appliqués, trims, and embroidery.

Ruffle and finishing: Cut and join eyelet edging as for Square Pillow ruffle, above. Cut lace to fit around patchwork piece, plus 1 inch; lap ends ½ inch and stitch to form ring. Offsetting the joins, with both right sides up, pin the lace ring over the eyelet ring, matching outer edges; machine-baste together. Then pin and baste the combined edgings to the patchwork pillow top and finish as for Square Pillow.

Heart Pillow

Pattern and layout: Enlarge the heart pattern (see page 45). Using pattern, cut heart-shaped foundation from Pellon fleece. Following the layout diagram (Figure 3), create the patchwork pillow top, trimming excess fabric even with edges of heart. Then, using lace appliqués, trims, and embroidery stitches, embellish as desired.

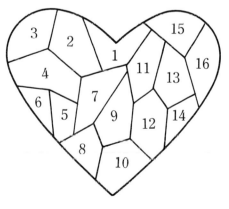

Figure 3

43

Figure 4

Edging: Allowing for ease, cut edging long enough to fit around heart plus ½ inch. Lap ends of edging and whipstitch together to form a ring. With right sides together and matching edges, pin edging around heart, placing seam at upper inside notch of heart and easing edging around lower point, as shown (Figure 4). Machine-baste ¼ inch from edge.

Finishing: Using pattern, cut backing. With right sides together, pin backing to patchwork heart all around, enclosing edging. Leaving an opening along one side for turning and stuffing, stitch top and backing together. Grade seam allowances, clip notch, trim point, and turn right side out. Stuff; then turn opening edges under and slipstitch the opening closed.

Color Guide

These pillows make use of medium to pale pastels in the beige, rose, pink, and gray families. For the square pillow, the master print is a large floral, which has been accented by embroidering over a few of the flowers. The purchased ruffle is off-white with contrast picot edging. The rectangular pillow uses muted prints and solids and features lace trims that were cut from antique linens. The eyelet ruffle is set off by rose-colored lace. Delicate colors and laces were combined to create the heart-shaped pillow, trimmed with antique hand-crocheted edging. (Instructions for the vest are on page 73.)

Each square = 2″

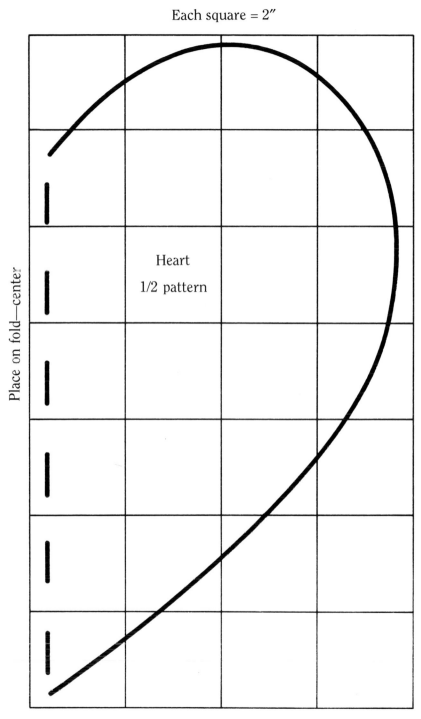

Place on fold—center

Heart
1/2 pattern

PATTERN FOR HEART PILLOW

Cabbage Rose Pillows

Sizes: With twisted satin cord (front), 16 × 16 inches; with welting (back), 15 × 15 inches; neck roll (center), 12 inches long (excluding ruffle) × 5 inches diameter

Materials for square pillows (enough for 2 pillows, either size)

Note: All fabrics are 45 inches wide.
½ yard master print
¼ yard each of 6 to 8 coordinating fabrics
½ yard Pellon fleece
Assorted lace trims (see "Basic Terms and Techniques")
Embroidery materials (see "Embroidery Techniques and Stitches")
½ yard backing fabric

For each satin-cord-trimmed pillow: 2 yards twisted satin cord, with flange
A few small beads
16-inch-square pillow form or polyester stuffing

For each welted pillow: 1¾ yards welting, ½ inch in diameter
Polyester stuffing

Directions

Note: All measurements include ¼-inch seam allowances.

Satin-Cord-Trimmed Pillow

Patchwork layout: For each pillow, cut a 16½-inch square of Pellon fleece for layout foundation. Then follow the instructions for Basic Layout, pages 17–19, to create a patchwork piece for the pillow top. Then, using trims, beads, and embroidery stitches, embellish entire layout as desired (see "Basic Terms and Techniques" and "Embroidery Techniques and Stitches").

Cord trim: Cut cord trim into 4 equal lengths. Beginning at one corner, and with twisted portion facing center, pin flange of each length of cord trim to right side of patchwork pillow top along one edge, allowing ends of cord trim to meet and extend at each corner, as shown (Figure 5). If flange is wider than ¼ inch, position so excess extends beyond edge of patchwork piece, to maintain ¼-inch seam allowance. Using a zipper/cording foot, machine-baste cord trim in place, starting and ending stitching just short of corners, as shown (Figure 5).

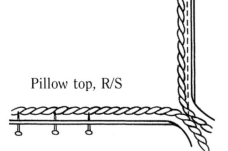

Pillow top, R/S

Figure 5

Finishing: From backing fabric cut a square the same size as patchwork pillow top. With right sides together and edges matching, pin top and backing together, enclosing cord. Still using zipper/cording foot, stitch around 4 corners (sewing across cord ends) and 3 sides, leaving an opening for turning and stuffing. Grade seam allowances, trim corners and excess cord, and turn right side out. Insert pillow form or stuff with polyester stuffing. Turn opening edges under and slipstitch opening closed.

Welted Pillow

Patchwork layout: Follow instructions for Satin-Cord-Trimmed Pillow, earlier, *except* cut Pellon fleece foundation 15½ inches square. Omit beads.

Welting: Allowing for ease at corners, cut welting to fit around patchwork square plus 1 inch. Matching unfinished edge of welting to edges of patchwork square, pin welting in place all around, rounding corners slightly and joining ends neatly (see page 26). Using a zipper/cording foot, machine-baste ¼ inch from edge all around.

Finishing: Follow instructions for Satin-Cord-Trimmed Pillow.

Materials for neck roll (enough for 2 pillows)

Note: All fabrics are 45 inches wide.
¼ yard each of 6 coordinating fabrics
Small amount muslin
½ yard Pellon fleece
Embroidery materials (see "Embroidery Techniques and Stitches")
Assorted lace trims and appliqués
1 yard pregathered muslin ruffling, about 2 inches wide
Polyester stuffing
Yardstick, pencil, compass

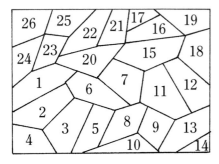

Figure 6

Directions

Note: All measurements include ¼-inch seam allowances.

Patchwork layout: Cut a rectangle of Pellon fleece 17¾ × 12½ inches for layout foundation. Following the layout diagram (Figure 6), create a patchwork layout. Using embroidery stitches and lace trims, embellish layout as desired.

Ruffles: Cut ruffling into 2 equal lengths. With right sides together and ruffles facing center, pin a ruffle to each *long* edge of the patchwork piece; machine-baste ruffles in place. Press seam allowances toward ruffles. Now, with right sides together, pin the *short* edges of the patchwork piece and the ends of the ruffles together as shown (Figure 7), leaving about 6 inches

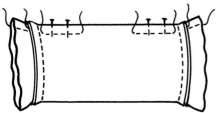

Figure 7

unpinned in the center for turning. Stitch where pinned (break stitching at intersecting seam allowances, leaving them free) to form a tube with a ruffle at each end. Press seam allowances open. Finish raw ends of ruffles with zigzag or overcast stitching. Do not turn yet.

Finishing: For pillow ends, using compass, draw two 5½-inch-diameter circles on muslin; cut out. Mark edge of each circle into quarters by folding and snipping a *small notch* into the seam allowance. Mark ends of ruffled patchwork tube in same way, using the seam as one of the marks. With right sides together, pin circular pillow ends in place, matching edges and markings, and enclosing ruffles, as shown (Figure 8). Stitch all around, being careful not to catch loose edges of ruffles in stitching. Grade and notch seam allowances and turn right side out. Stuff pillow, turn opening edges under, and slipstitch the opening closed.

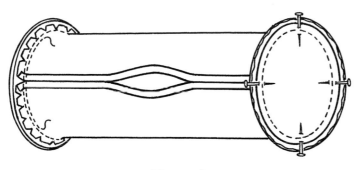

Figure 8

Color Guide

Cabbage roses play an important role in the design of the two square pillows shown here. Both pillows use the same master print of cabbage roses, which are highlighted with overembroidery. Colors are mainly dusty greens and roses, repeated in the coordinating smaller prints and solids. White accents are provided by lace trims and small pearly beads. Also note the embroidered heart and the overembellishment of the cabbage rose with the buttonhole stitch. The fabrics and trims used for the neck roll are small prints that repeat the color scheme of the larger pillows.

Victorian Teacup Quilt

Size: 52 × 52 inches

Materials

Note: All fabrics are 45 inches wide.
1 yard master print
¼ yard each of 10 to 12 coordinating fabrics, both prints and solids
1½ yards contrasting solid for inside border
1⅝ yards second contrasting solid for outside border and binding
3¾ yards Pellon fleece
Embroidery materials, including gold metallic thread (see "Embroidery Techniques and Stitches")
Assorted lace trims and bugle beads (see "Basic Terms and Techniques")
3 yards backing fabric
Paper for patterns
Ruler, yardstick, pencil

Directions

Note: All measurements, except where indicated, include ¼-inch seam allowances. When joining pieces, place right sides together and stitch ¼-inch seams; press seam allowances to one side unless instructed otherwise.

Patterns: To make pattern for patchwork block, first draw and cut out an 11-inch square. Fold in half vertically, then fold in half horizontally to mark center of each side; unfold. Connect the center points of 2 adjacent sides, then connect the center points of the opposite adjacent sides, as shown (Figure 11). Cut away the 2 triangles that result (Figure 12), saving one to use as a corner

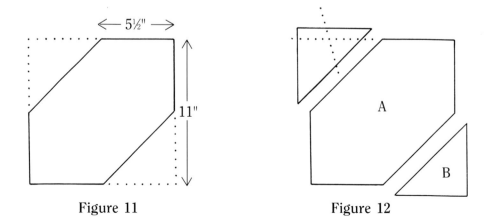

Figure 11   Figure 12

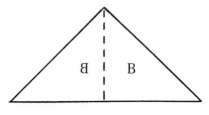

Figure 13

triangle pattern. Mark the larger, hexagonal piece "A" and the triangular piece "B." Using pattern B, make a large triangle pattern as follows: Trace around diagonal and 1 straight side of pattern, then flop pattern and trace around same 2 sides, as shown (Figure 13). Cut out. To use these patterns, follow the cutting instructions below, *adding ¼-inch seam allowances all around.* Also draw an 8⅜-inch square (includes seam allowances) for teacup block; mark this pattern "C." Trace actual-size cup-and-saucer design (dot marks center) (see page 59).

Cutting: ***From Pellon fleece:*** Cut 16 from pattern A, 4 from pattern B, and 4 large triangles (remember to add seam allowances). From pattern C cut 5. Reserve remaining Pellon fleece for borders. Select a light solid or subtle print for patterns B and C. Use Pellon fleece pieces as patterns. ***From selected fabric:*** Cut 4 B, 5 C, and 4 large triangles. ***From first contrasting solid:*** Cut 4 lengthwise strips each 1½ × 53 inches for inner border. ***From second contrasting solid:*** Cut 4 lengthwise strips each 3½ × 53 inches for outer border. Also cut and piece enough 1½-inch-wide bias strips (see page 29) to measure about 6½ yards. When ready to bind edge, prepare strip for binding as directed on page 29.

Any leftovers of the preceding fabrics may be used for the patchwork blocks.

Patchwork blocks (make 16): For each block, use 1 Pellon fleece A piece for the foundation. See "Basic Terms and Techniques" for basic layout techniques; then, using the master print and 6 to 8 other fabrics, follow the layout given here (Figure 14) to create 16 patchwork blocks. Always include 2 or 3 patches of the master print, but you may vary the other fabrics so that no two blocks are alike. Now, using embroidery stitches, along with touches of lace and beads, embellish each block as desired (see "Embroidery Techniques and Stitches").

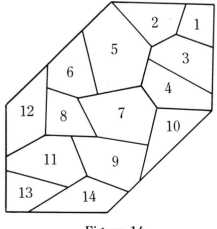

Figure 14

54

Teacup blocks: Note that these blocks (cut from pattern C) are set diagonally. Mark center of each block, then transfer (see page 26) a cup-and-saucer design to each block, matching center markings. Layer onto Pellon square; embroider with whipped running stitch through all layers (page 34), using metallic thread for outer edge of saucer and rim of cup. Embroider a different flower motif (pages 34–39) on each cup.

Assembly: Back each fabric triangle with Pellon fleece and machine-baste. Arrange all blocks and triangles as shown in Assembly Diagram (Figure 15). Then, beginning with one teacup block, join a patchwork block to each edge, beginning and ending each seam ¼ inch from corner, as shown (Figures 16a, b). Join adjacent edges of patchwork blocks, as shown (Figures 16c, d). When 4 such units have been completed, arrange them as shown (Figure 17); first join edges to center teacup block, then adjacent edges of units, then add remaining pieces as follows: large triangles, small corner triangles.

Borders: Join an inside border strip to an outside border strip along one long edge; repeat with remaining strips. Cut a strip of Pellon fleece to fit each joined strip; then back strips as for blocks and triangles.

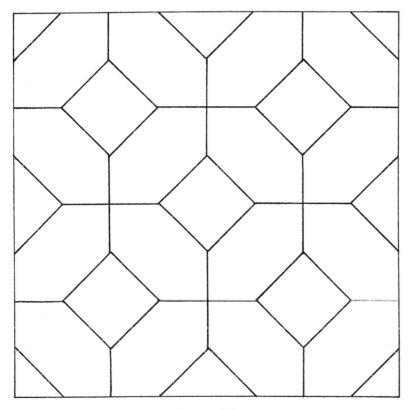

Figure 15

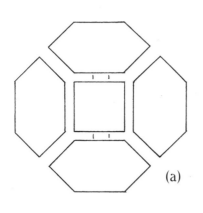

(a)

Stop at ¼"

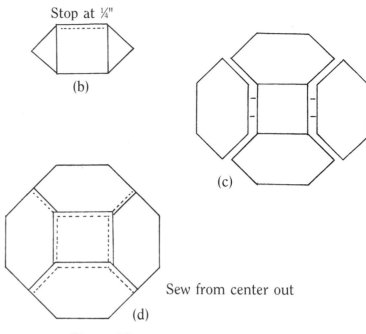

(b)

(c)

(d)

Sew from center out

Figure 16

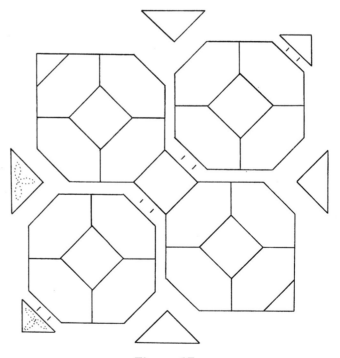

Figure 17

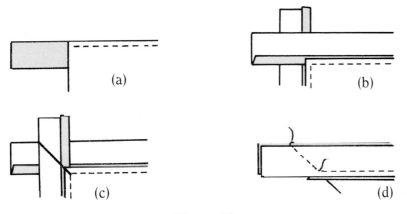

Figure 18

Joining borders to quilt top: With right sides together and matching center of strip edge to center of quilt edge, pin inner edge of a border strip to one edge of quilt (with strip ends extending). Stitch, starting and ending ¼ inch from quilt corners, as shown (Figure 18a). Repeat on remaining 3 sides.

Mitered corners: Place quilt flat, wrong side up, lapping border strip ends as shown (Figure 18b). At one corner, mark 45-degree diagonal line on upper strip end from corner seamline to outer edge as shown (Figure 18c). Reverse lapping to mark under strip. Fold quilt corner in half diagonally, right sides together, with ends matching and seam allowances pressed away from borders as shown (Figure 18d). Align and pin together marked lines on borders. Stitch along line and trim excess fabric to leave ¼ inch seam allowance. Repeat on remaining corners.

Backing: Cut backing fabric into 2 equal lengths. Then follow instructions on page 28 to piece the backing, assemble the quilt layers, and baste the layers together. Trim backing to same size as quilt top.

Quilting: Trace the leaf template (see page 60) and transfer the leaf motif to each triangle as shown (Figure 19). Hand-quilt or machine-quilt. Then machine-quilt along all seams, directly over the seamlines, through all layers.

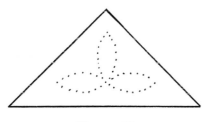

Figure 19

Scallops: Using the pattern on page 60, make a paper template (see pages 27–28) and mark 9 scallops along each edge as shown (Figure 20); aligning straight edge of guide with outer edge of border, begin marking at center of each edge, connecting corner scallops gracefully. Stitch along all marked curves, through all layers; then trim ¼ inch outside stitching.

Finishing: Prepare binding as directed on page 29. Open out binding and, with right sides together and edges matching, beginning at center of one side, pin binding to quilt top, clipping quilt at notches between scallops. Stitch, pivoting at clipped corners. Fold binding in half along pressed fold and pin to back of quilt, forming small pleats at base of scallops. Slipstitch in place, joining ends neatly (see page 27).

Color Guide

Pretty pastels, mostly echoing the rose and green of the master print, are the main colors here, accented with beige and white. Off-white lace bands and beads are used sparingly to enhance the embroidery, also done in mostly pastel shades. The teacups and saucers are outlined in whipped running stitches, using pink, white, and gold metallic threads to simulate the gold rims on fine china. The matching tea cozy features shirred welting, made from the master print.

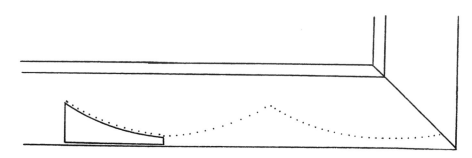

Figure 20

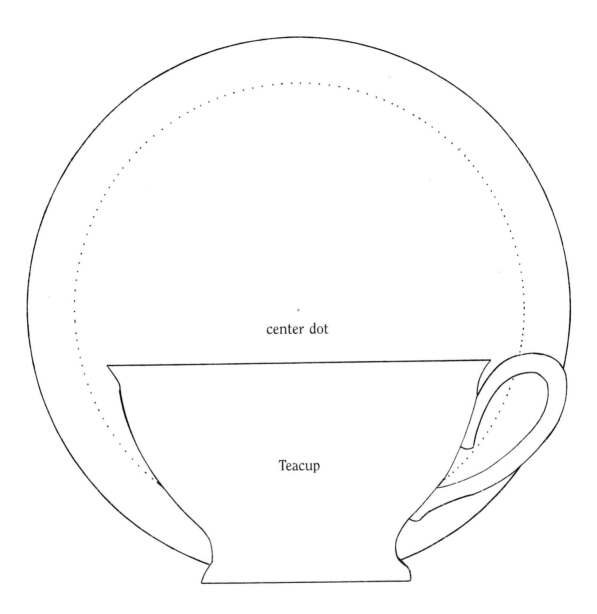

center dot

Teacup

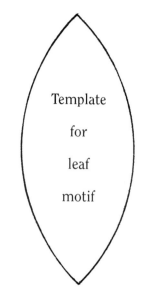

Template

for

leaf

motif

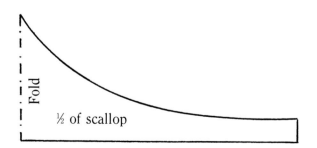

Fold

½ of scallop

Tea Cozy

- -

Size: 13 × 13 inches

Materials

Note: All fabrics are 45 inches wide.

½ yard master print (includes enough for backing, binding, and welting)

Small amounts of 6 to 8 coordinating fabrics (or use leftovers from Victorian Teacup Quilt, earlier)

½ yard Pellon fleece

½ yard lining fabric

Lace trims and embroidery materials similar to those used for Victorian Teacup Quilt

1 yard filler cable cord, ¾ inch in diameter

Paper for patterns

Ruler, yardstick, pencil

Directions

Note: All measurements include ¼-inch seam allowances.

Pattern and cutting: On paper draw a 13-inch square, fold in half vertically, and mark as shown (Figure 21). Cut away small section outside marked curve. Open folded piece and use as a pattern to cut: 2 from Pellon fleece, 2 from lining fabric, and 1 from master print (for backing).

Also, from Pellon fleece and from 1 fabric cut one 8⅜-inch square each (including ¼-inch seam allowance) for teacup block. Save remaining master print for patchwork, welting, and binding.

Patchwork front: Transfer cup-and-saucer design to the fabric square, back the block with the Pellon fleece and embroider as for Victorian Teacup Quilt blocks. Center the teacup block on one of the Pellon fleece shapes, as shown (Figure 22); pin in place. Now follow the layout given here (Figure 23) to cre-

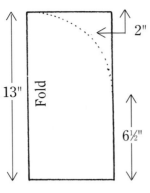

Figure 21

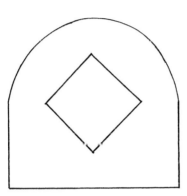

Figure 22

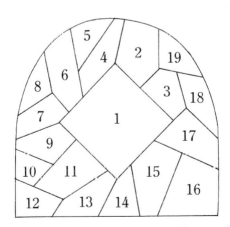

Figure 23

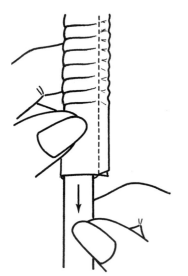

Figure 24

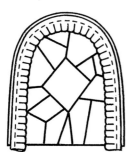

Figure 25

ate the patchwork front, using the master print and other fabrics. Where patches meet teacup block, interlock the edges (pages 16–17) and lap them ¼ inch over the teacup block. Using embroidery stitches and lace trims, embellish the patchwork front as desired.

Shirred welting: From reserved master print cut and piece enough 3-inch-wide bias strips (see page 29) to measure about 2 yards. Starting at one end, enclose filler cord in bias strip, right side out, matching long edges of strip. Using a zipper/cording foot, stitch next to, but not through, the cord for several inches. With presser foot lowered and needle in fabric, grasp the stitched portion behind the needle in one hand and with the other hand pull gently on the cord, gathering the stitched portion, as shown (Figure 24). Continue in this manner until the entire cord is covered with shirred fabric. Adjust gathers evenly, then stitch across each end to secure.

With shirred portion facing center, beginning and ending at bottom, pin seam allowances of shirred welting to the patchwork cozy front; using a zipper/cording foot, machine-baste, as shown (Figure 25).

Assembly: Back the backing fabric with the remaining piece of Pellon fleece. With right sides together, pin backing over front, enclosing welting. Using zipper/cording foot, stitch around curved edge. Trim any excess welting, grade seam allowances, and turn right side out.

Lining: With right sides together, stitch lining sections around curved edge, leaving bottom edge open. Do not turn. Insert lining into tea cozy, matching side seams. Pin lower edges of lining to cozy and machine-baste together. If desired, turn entire piece inside out and tack lining to cozy at intervals along seams; turn right side out.

Finishing: From leftover master print, cut and piece enough 1½-inch-wide bias strips to fit around lower edge of cozy. Prepare strip for binding as described on page 29. Beginning at center back, open one edge of strip, and, with right sides together, pin binding to outside of cozy all around lower edge. Stitch in place, joining ends neatly. Fold binding over edge to inside of cozy, pin in place, and slipstitch.

Tasseled Victorian Table Cover

Size: 44 × 44 inches

Materials

Note: All fabrics are 45 inches wide.

⅜ to ½ yard each of 6 to 7 luxury fabrics such as moiré, satin, jacquard, and faille, in solid colors

1¼ yards Pellon fleece

1¼ yards backing fabric

Embroidery materials (see "Embroidery Techniques and Stitches")

Assorted lace trims and appliqués, ribbons, seed and bugle beads, and decorative buttons (see "Basic Terms and Techniques" and "Embroidery Techniques and Stitches")

5¼ yards twisted satin cord trim, with flange, ½ inch in diameter

Four 3-inch tassels

Directions

Note: All measurements include ¼-inch seam allowances.

Patchwork layout: From Pellon fleece cut a 44½-inch square for layout foundation. Then follow the instructions for Advanced Layout, page 21, to create a patchwork piece for table cover top. Using lace bands, edgings and appliques, ribbons, embroidery stitches, and beads and buttons, embellish entire layout as desired (see "Basic Terms and Techniques" and "Embroidery Techniques and Stitches").

Cord trim: Cut cord trim into 4 equal lengths. Beginning at one corner, and with twisted portion facing center, pin flange of each length of cord trim to right side of patchwork along one edge, allowing ends of cord trim to meet and extend at each corner, as shown (Figure 26). Seam allowance is ¼ inch; if flange is wider than ¼ inch, position so excess extends beyond edge of patchwork piece. Using a zipper/cording foot, machine-baste cord trim in place, starting and ending stitching just short of corners, as shown (Figure 26).

Assembly: Trim backing fabric to same size as patchwork top. With right sides together, pin backing to top, enclosing cord trim. Using zipper/cording foot, stitch around 4 corners (sewing across cord ends) and 3 sides, leaving an opening along one edge for turning. Trim corners and excess cord, grade seam allowances, and turn right side out. Turn edges of opening ¼ inch to wrong side and slipstitch opening closed. Sew a tassel at each corner.

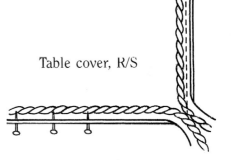

Table cover, R/S

Figure 26

Tasseled Pillow

- -

Size: 19 × 14 inches

Materials

Note: All fabrics are 45 inches wide.

¼ yard each of 6 or 7 fabrics the same as or similar to those used for Tasseled Victorian Table Cover earlier

½ yard Pellon fleece

Embroidery materials (see "Embroidery Techniques and Stitches")

Assorted trims, including lace, narrow ribbon, and beads

2 yards twisted satin cord trim, with flange, 1½ inch in diameter

½ yard backing fabric

Polyester stuffing

Four 3-inch tassels

Directions

Note: All measurements include ¼-inch seam allowances.

Patchwork layout: Cut a rectangle of Pellon fleece 19½ × 14½ inches for layout foundation. Use the instructions for Basic Layout, pages 17–19, as a guide for creating a rectangular patchwork pillow top. Then, using trims, beads, and embroidery stitches, embellish layout as desired (see "Basic Terms and Techniques" and "Embroidery Techniques and Stitches").

Cord trim: Follow instructions for Tasseled Victorian Table Cover.

Finishing: From backing fabric cut a rectangle the same size as patchwork pillow top. With right sides together, pin backing to top all around. Using zipper/cording foot, stitch around 4 corners and 3 sides, leaving an opening for turning and stuffing, and rounding corners very slightly. Grade seam allowances, trim corners and excess cord, and turn right side out. Stuff pillow. Turn opening edges under and slipstitch opening closed. Sew a tassel at each corner.

Color Guide

The table cover is done in muted shades of rose and green, with accents of black and off-white. Embellishment is quite lavish, with bands and appliqués of white, black, and ecru lace, black and rose ribbons, and embroidery, some of it enhanced by beads and novelty buttons. The twisted cord trim and tassels are black. The tasseled pillow is intended to coordinate closely with the table cover, using several of the same fabrics, as well as the same twisted cord trim and tassels. The pillow embellishments are similar, though somewhat simpler.

Victorian Wearables and Accessories

Sweatshirt with Patchwork Yoke

Materials

Sweatshirt in desired size
¼ yard each of 7 or 8 coordinating fabrics
Embroidery materials (see "Embroidery Techniques and Stitches")
Ruler, yardstick, chalk or washable marker

Directions

Preparation of garment: Remove labels and launder sweatshirt. Cut sweatshirt open along side seams and sleeve (underarm) seams, to within 6 inches of cuffs, as shown (Figure 1). (If there are no side seams, lay garment flat and press a crease where each side seam would fall, then cut along crease.)

Marking of yoke position: Open out sweatshirt so neck opening is at center and front, back, and sleeves lie flat, as shown (Figure 2). Using ruler and chalk, measure 10 inches from base of center front neckband and mark front; repeat for center back and sleeves, as shown (Figure 2). Connect marks for position of yoke edges (Figure 2).

Patchwork layout: See "Basic Terms and Techniques" for basic layout techniques, including preparing fabric strips, forming the patchwork, and interlocking edges. Then follow the layout given here (Figure 3) to create the patchwork yoke. Note that instead of Pellon fleece, the garment itself acts as the foundation. Be sure that all patches at neck and outer edges are neatly interlocked. Now, using embroidery stitches, embellish entire layout as desired (see "Embroidery Techniques and Stitches").

Finishing: With right sides together, pin side and sleeve edges together and stitch, using an overlock or serging stitch. Alternatively, you can stitch scant ¼-inch seams, then zigzag-stitch the edges of the seam allowances together.

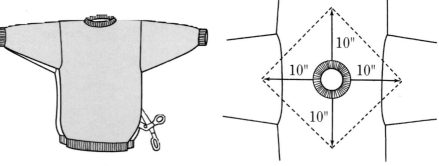

Figure 1   Figure 2

Patchwork Sweatshirt Cardigan

Materials

Sweatshirt in desired size
1½ yards master print (includes enough for lining)
¼ yard each of 8 to 10 coordinating fabrics
¼ yard fabric to match sweatshirt, for front band
¼ yard Pellon fleece
Embroidery materials (see "Embroidery Techniques and Stitches")
9 buttons
Ruler, yardstick, chalk or washable marker

Directions

Note: Seam allowance is ¼ inch.

Follow instructions for Sweatshirt with Patchwork Yoke, page 68, to prepare garment and mark yoke position, *but* do not mark V-shaped yoke at center front, since entire front will be covered with patchwork.

Patchwork layout: See "Basic Terms and Techniques" for basic layout techniques, including methods for preparing fabric strips, forming the patchwork, and interlocking edges. Then follow the layout given in Figure 4 to create the

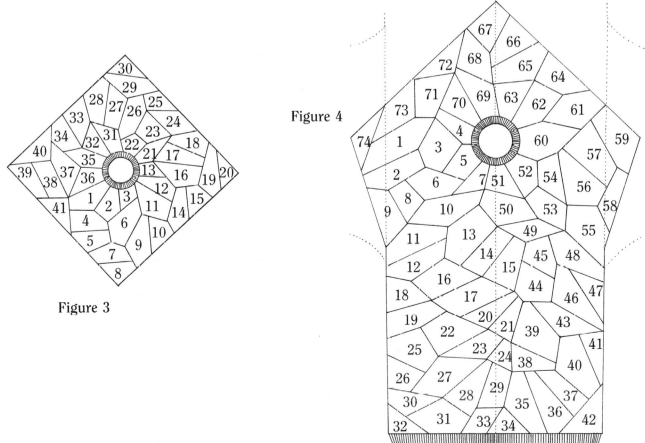

Figure 3

Figure 4

patchwork design, covering entire front and forming a V-shaped yoke in back. Note that instead of Pellon fleece, the garment itself acts as the foundation. Be sure that all patches at neck and outer edges of yoke are neatly interlocked; it is not necessary to interlock at side edges of front. Now, using embroidery stitches, embellish entire layout as desired (see "Embroidery Techniques and Stitches").

Fold front section in half lengthwise to determine center; mark center front line, as shown (Figure 4).

Lining: Turn sweatshirt inside out and place on flat surface (a padded ironing board is ideal) with wrong side of front facing you. Stretch the ribbed band at the lower edge of the front and pin it to the board. Measure length and width of front, then cut a piece of lining fabric to these measurements, adding an extra inch or two all around. Now pin the lining to the wrong side of the garment front, trimming to fit the size and shape, clipping curve at neck edge, and turning raw edges under, as shown (Figure 5). Lining should fit a bit

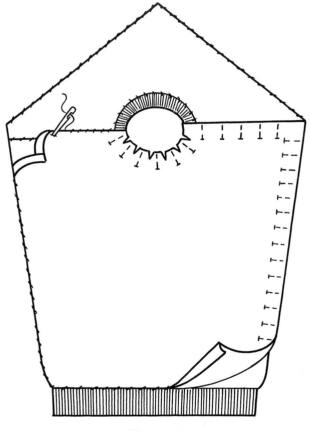

Figure 5

loosely, since the sweatshirt is stretchy. Unpin ribbed band and rearrange garment on board so wrong side of back yoke faces you. Cut remaining lining fabric to size and shape of back yoke (again allowing a little extra all around) and pin in place. Front lining should lap over back-yoke lining at shoulders. Slipstitch entire lining in place (Figure 5), taking small stitches but keeping them fairly loose, to allow for stretching.

Front bands: With right side up, machine-stitch ¼ inch away from each side of marked center front line, through all layers, then cut front apart along center front line. Measure length of center front opening, including neckband and bottom ribbed band. From matching fabric cut 2 crosswise strips each 3½ inches wide by the length measured above plus ½ inch. From Pellon fleece cut 2 strips the same length and 1¾ inches wide. Matching both ends and a long edge, pin 1 fleece strip to a fabric strip; machine-baste across ends and along long edge. Fold strip in half lengthwise with right sides together; stitch across ends only. Trim corners, grade seam allowances, turn right side out, and press. Repeat with remaining strip.

With right sides together, beginning at neck edge, pin one open edge of front band along front opening edge, as shown (Figure 6). Stitch in place. Grade seam allowances, then press toward band and press band away from seam, facing center. Repeat with other front band. On wrong side of front, turn raw edges of front bands under, pin to lining, and slipstitch in place, as shown (Figure 7).

Mark position of buttonholes on right front band, placing first and last buttonholes ¾ inch from upper and lower ends of band and spacing the rest evenly between. Make buttonholes.

Finishing: Sew side and sleeve seams as for Sweatshirt with Patchwork Yoke, page 68. Sew buttons to left front band opposite buttonholes.

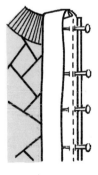

Figure 6

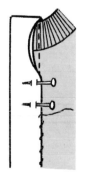

Figure 7

Color Guide

Shades of rose, muted blues, and a crisp black reflect the colors of the floral master print with a black background. Black trim outlines the patchwork fronts and matches the black sweatshirt. The embroidery threads repeat the colors of the patches, perked up with bright pink and soft yellow.

Lined Baseball Jacket

Materials

Note: All fabrics are 45 inches wide.
Bought baseball jacket pattern (choose one with patch pockets and a lining)
½ yard master print
¼ yard each 7 to 10 coordinating fabrics, prints and solids
Approximately 1½ yards solid fabric for back and sleeves (see pattern pieces)
Lining fabric (see pattern envelope)
3 yards Pellon fleece
Plastic separating zipper (see pattern envelope)
1 set purchased rib-knit neckband, cuffs, and waistband
Embroidery materials (see "Embroidery Techniques and Stitches")
Yardstick and chalk

Directions

Patchwork layout: Cut 2 rectangles of Pellon fleece just large enough to accommodate jacket front pattern piece. Then follow the instructions for Intermediate Layout, page 20, to create 2 patchwork rectangles (patchwork designs do not need to be indentical). Using pocket pattern piece, create 2 more patchwork rectangles in same way. Using embroidery stitches, embellish each patchwork piece (see "Embroidery Techniques and Stitches").

Cutting: Using pattern pieces and following cutting diagrams from pattern instruction sheet where applicable, cut pieces as follows: *From large patchwork pieces:* 2 jacket fronts, 1 in reverse; *from small patchwork pieces:* 2 pockets, 1 in reverse; *from solid:* back and sleeves; *from Pellon fleece:* back and sleeves; *from lining fabric:* pockets, fronts, back, and sleeves.

Marking: Transfer any pattern markings. Also mark quilting lines on back and sleeves as follows: Fold back in half lengthwise to determine center; mark at top and bottom, then, using yardstick and chalk, connect marks. Continue to mark parallel lines 2½ inches apart on each side of center line, out to side edges. Mark sleeves in same way.

Assembly: Pin corresponding Pellon fleece sections and lining to the wrong side of back and sleeve sections, then machine-quilt through all layers ¼ inch away from each side of marked lines. Baste each front to its lining. Follow pattern instructions for making pockets (line so that all edges are finished); stitch to fronts through lining. Follow pattern to assemble jacket and to apply knit bands and zipper. For a neater finish inside the jacket, bind all the raw edges, using leftover lining fabric for the binding strips (see page 29).

Color Guide

Although the master print is a bold red and green print on a black background, the dominating color in this baseball jacket is navy blue, used for the back, sleeves, and knit bands, as well as in the patchwork design itself. Other prints and solids include red, green, and rose. The embroidery, in lighter shades, is kept simple to enhance rather than compete with the patchwork design.

Victorian Vest

Materials

Note: All fabrics are 45 inches wide.
Commercial vest pattern (choose one that is constructed with a lining)
½ yard master print
¼ yard each of 6 or 7 coordinating fabrics
1 yard Pellon fleece or muslin
Embroidery materials (see "Embroidery Techniques and Stitches")
Assorted lace and trims
Lining fabric (see pattern envelope)
Fabric for vest back (see pattern piece)
1 package corded piping (optional)
Decorative buttons and narrow ribbon (optional)

Directions

Patchwork layout: Using pattern piece for vest fronts, cut foundations from Pellon fleece (or from muslin, if a more lightweight garment is desired). See "Basic Terms and Techniques" for basic layout technique, then follow the diagrams given here (Figure 8) to create the patchwork vest fronts. Using lace, trims, and embroidery stitches, embellish vest fronts as desired.

Assembly: If piping is to be used, cut it to fit the edges to be piped, adding an extra inch or two. With edges matching, pin piping tape to right side of vest fronts, easing piping around curves and clipping the tape at corners. Using a zipper/cording foot, machine-baste in place.

Use pattern pieces to cut vest back and lining. Follow sewing instructions given with pattern to complete vest. If buttons permit, sew in place first, then draw ribbons through holes and tie into bows.

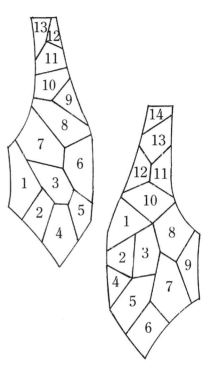

Figure 8

Collection of Purses

Easy Purse

Size: 6½ × 8½ inches

Materials

Small amounts 6 to 7 fabrics
9- × 13½-inch piece of Pellon fleece
Two 9- × 7-inch pieces of lining fabric
Embroidery materials (see "Embroidery Techniques and Stitches") and seed beads
2-inch strip Velcro® tape for closure
Optional: No. 8 pearl cotton for twisted rope handle

Directions

Note: All measurements include ¼-inch seam allowances.

Patchwork layout: See "Basic Terms and Techniques" for basic layout technique. Then, working over the top half of the Pellon fleece foundation, follow the layout given here (Figure 9) to create the patchwork for the front of the purse. Rotate the foundation 180 degrees and, using the same layout, create the patchwork for the back; fold or interlock the pieces as appropriate where the two layouts meet. Using embroidery stitches and clusters of beads, embellish the entire layout as desired (see "Embroidery Techniques and Stitches"). With right sides together, fold completed patchwork piece in half crosswise, pin side edges together, and stitch. Trim lower corners, grade seam allowances, and turn right side out.

Lining: With right sides together, pin and stitch side edges of lining together (leave lower edge open), as shown (Figure 10); do not turn. With right sides together and side seams matching, slip lining over purse and pin top edges of purse and lining together all around; stitch as shown (Figure 11). Grade seam allowances.

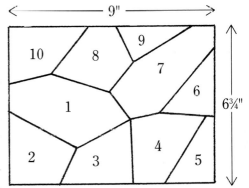

Figure 9

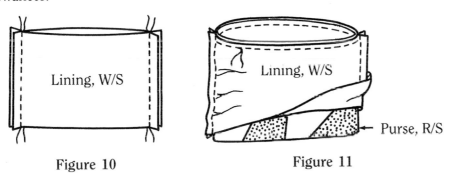

Figure 10   Figure 11

Pull lining up away from purse. Turn open lower edges of lining ¼ inch to the wrong side and pin together. Slipstitch or machine-stitch close to turned edges. Tuck lining down into purse.

Finishing: On lining, mark position for each half of Velcro tape, about 1 inch below upper edge of purse and centered between side seams. Sew in place. If desired, make a twisted rope handle using 12 lengths of No. 8 pearl cotton, each 2 yards long, in any desired color combination, as follows: Knot strands together at one end and attach the knotted end to a door handle or drawer pull. Twist and twist strands clockwise until strands form a tight cable, then fold in half, letting cable twist on itself. Knot ends and trim, leaving a 1-inch tassel. Sew knots to side seams of lining, 1½ inches below top edge.

Clutch Purse

Size: Approximately 8½ × 11½ inches each

Materials

Small amounts 6 to 8 fabrics, both prints and solids
12- × 26-inch piece of Pellon fleece
½ yard lining fabric
Embroidery materials (see "Embroidery Techniques and Stitches")

Directions

Note: All measurements include ¼-inch seam allowances.

Patchwork layout: See "Basic Terms and Techniques" for basic layout technique. Follow the layout given here (Figure 12). Mark the fold lines on the Pellon fleece as shown on the layout, dividing the piece into thirds. Trim the fleece at upper left corner as shown to form a slanted flap. Then follow the layout to create the patchwork piece for your purse. Using embroidery stitches, embellish the patchwork piece as desired (see "Embroidery Techniques and Stitches").

Lining: Cut lining fabric 1 inch larger all around than patchwork piece. Press all edges of lining ¼ inch to wrong side. Center patchwork, right side up, over lining, *wrong side up.* Beginning at one long edge, fold lining over edge to patchwork front, forming a ¾-inch-wide binding. Pin in place, mitering or folding corners neatly. Fold inside top edge (the short, straight end) of binding last. With patchwork side facing up, stitch binding in place, close to both edges.

Finishing: Form clutch purse by folding along previously marked lines, with lining on inside. Pin side edges together and stitch together through all layers, close to outer edges.

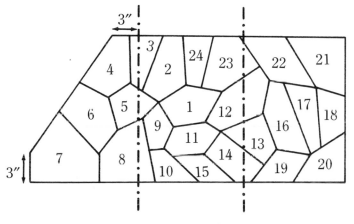

Figure 12

Crossover Shoulder Bag

Size: 10 × 11 inches

Materials

Note: All fabrics are 45 inches wide.
½ yard master print (includes enough for lining)
Small amounts 4 or 5 coordinating fabrics
⅜ yard Pellon fleece
Embroidery materials (see "Embroidery Techniques and Stitches")
1 package corded piping
2-inch strip Velcro® tape for closure
Approximately 30-inch "gold" chain
No. 3 pearl cotton for tassels
2 decorative buttons
Paper for pattern

Directions

Note: All measurements include ¼-inch seam allowances.

Pattern: On paper, draw a rectangle 10½ inches wide × 11½ inches high. Mark center of top edge, then draw a line as shown (Figure 13). Cut off area above marked line and use remaining piece as a pattern.

Cutting: Using pattern, from Pellon fleece cut 2 pieces for layout foundation; from master print cut 2 pieces for lining. Remaining master print may be used for patchwork layout.

Patchwork layout: See "Basic Terms and Techniques" for basic layout technique. Follow layouts given here (Figure 14) to create patchwork pieces for front and back of bag. Using embroidery stitches, embellish patchwork as desired (see "Embroidery Techniques and Stitches").

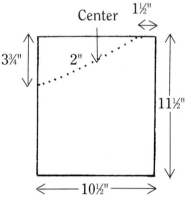

Figure 13

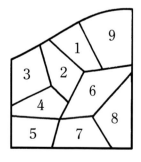 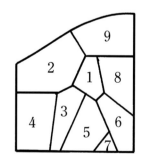

Figure 14

Piping: With edges matching, pin piping flange to right side of each patchwork piece as shown (Figure 15), easing piping and clipping flange around curves; at lower edges of sides, ease piping off edge of patchwork so that the cord crosses the seam line. Using a zipper/cording foot, machine-baste in place, as shown (Figure 15). With right sides together, pin lower edges of bag front and back together; stitch. Trim corners and grade seam allowances. Press seam allowances open.

Lining: With right sides together, pin lower edges of lining together. Leaving center 6 inches open for turning, stitch seam. Press seam allowances open and opening edges under. With right sides together, pin lining to patchwork piece; using a zipper/cording foot, stitch in place all around. Turn bag right side out through opening in lining. Bring opening edges of lining together and slip-stitch in place.

Finishing: Fold bag in half along bottom seam, with lining inside. Using zipper/cording foot, stitch side edges together, as shown (Figure 16). On lining, mark position of Velcro tapes inside center top and sew in place.

Tassels and chain: For each tassel, cut 24 strands of No. 3 pearl cotton, each 7 inches long. Holding strands together, draw through end link of chain and fold in half, evening out ends; with another strand of pearl cotton, wrap and tie tassel ½ inch from chain link. Trim ends even. Repeat at other end of chain. On bag front, position knot of one tassel 1 inch below top edge of bag and 2 inches in from side. Back the knot on the lining side with a button and sew the knot securely in place on the patchwork as you sew through the holes of the button on the lining side. Repeat with other end of chain and other button on back of bag.

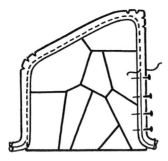

Figure 15

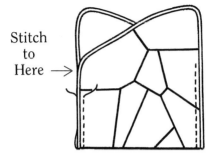

Stitch to Here →

Figure 16

Victorian Christmas

Patc
niqu
2) to
bon:
"Em

Asse
each
the
not
corr

the

this joined strip; pin and machine-baste the fleece to the back of the joined strip. Now join the upper edge of this piece to the lower edge of the tree/background piece, as shown (Figure 6).

Star: With fusible web underneath, position star on panel at top of tree. Following web manufacturer's directions, fuse star in place. Using matching pearl cotton, work blanket stitch all around star.

Borders (refer to Assembly Diagram [Figure 7]): Join a red inside border strip to each side edge of the tree panel, then join red top and bottom inside borders. For outside borders, first back each fabric strip with a Pellon fleece strip cut to the same size, then join outside borders in same sequence as inside borders. Trim any uneven edges and press all seams onto red borders. Using yardstick and chalk, mark quilting lines radiating from star and vertically on tree trunk, as shown (Figure 7).

Finishing: Cut backing the same size as front. If desired, add a rod pocket to back for hanging (see page 27). With *wrong* sides together and edges matching, pin backing to front. Baste the layers together as directed on page 28. Machine-quilt directly over all seamlines. Then, using metallic gold thread, hand-quilt along marked quilting lines on the tree background and around the star. Using black thread, hand-quilt along marked lines on tree trunk. *Binding:* From reserved dark print fabric, cut and piece enough 1½-inch-wide bias strips (see page 29) to measure about 5½ yards; prepare strip for binding. Open out one pressed edge of strip. With right sides together and raw edges matching, pin binding to quilt top all around. Stitch, mitering corners and joining ends neatly (see page 27). Fold binding over edge to backing, pin in place, and slipstitch.

4¾"

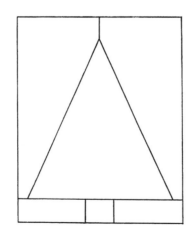

Figure 6

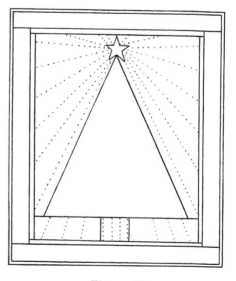

Figure 7

STAR PATTERN FOR CHRISTMAS TREE WALL HANGING

Christmas Table Runner and Tea Cozy

Sizes: Runner, 13 × 39 inches; cozy, 14 × 14 inches

Materials (for both)

Note: All fabrics are 45 inches wide.
½ yard master print
¼ yard each of 7 or 8 coordinating fabrics
1¼ yards Pellon fleece
Embroidery materials (see "Embroidery Techniques and Stitches")
1 yard backing fabric
½ yard lining fabric (for tea cozy only)
4 yards purchased wide bias tape for binding
3 tassels
Paper for pattern

Directions

Note: All measurements include ¼-inch seam allowances.

Runner

Patchwork layout: From Pellon fleece cut a 13- × 39-inch rectangle for foundation. Shape pointed ends the same as for the Victorian Table Runner on page 50. See "Basic Terms and Techniques" for basic layout technique, then follow the layout in Figure 10 on page 50 to create the patchwork table runner top. Using assorted colors and stitches, embroider the layout as desired (see "Basic Terms and Techniques" and "Embroidery Techniques and Stitches").

Finishing: From backing fabric cut a piece the same size as the patchwork top. With wrong sides together and edges matching, pin top and backing together. Machine-baste edge all around. Cut binding to fit around runner plus 6 inches. Open out one fold of binding. With right sides together, binding toward center, match edges and pin binding to runner top all around, mitering corners and joining ends neatly (see page 27). Stitch in place. Fold binding in half and pin to backing all around. Slipstitch in place. Sew tassels to points.

Color Guide

All items in the photo are made from the same fabrics, in "dusty" Christmas colors. The master print is a burgundy and beige paisley print on a green background. Other fabrics include miniature checks, plaids, and prints in similar tones. Contrasting embroidery and off-white lace and crochet trims complete the picture. Both the table runner and the tea cozy are bound in green and sport green tassels.

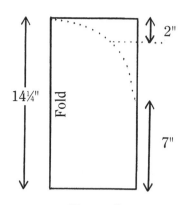

Figure 8

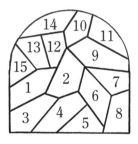

Figure 9

Cozy

Pattern: On paper draw a 14¼-inch square, fold in half vertically, and mark as shown (Figure 8). Cut away the small section outside marked curve. Open folded piece and use as a pattern to cut 4 Pellon fleece shapes. Set aside 3 of the shapes for later use.

Patchwork layout: Using remaining shaped piece as a foundation, create a patchwork layout to match the table runner, following the layout given here (Figure 9). Embroider as desired.

Finishing: Using one of the reserved Pellon fleece dome shapes as a pattern, cut 2 pieces from lining fabric and 1 piece from backing fabric. Pin 1 Pellon fleece piece to the wrong side of the backing piece; machine-baste all around a scant ¼ inch from edges. Now, with right sides together, pin the patchwork piece and the backing together around the curved edges only, leaving the straight bottom edge open. Stitch; then grade and notch seam allowances and turn right side out. Press lightly.

Back each lining piece with Pellon fleece in same way as for backing. Then, with right sides together, pin lining sections together around curved edges only. Stitch; grade and notch seam allowances but do not turn. Matching seams, insert lining into cozy. Pin bottom edges of lining to bottom edges of cozy, then machine-baste a scant ¼ inch from edge. Bind this edge in same way as for table runner. Sew tassel to center top of cozy.

Family Christmas Stockings

Sizes (height, from heel to top): Dad's, 15 inches; Mom's, 13 inches; child's, 10 inches

Materials (enough for one set)

Note: All fabrics are 45 inches wide.
⅝ yard master print (includes enough for backing)
¼ yard each of 7 or 8 coordinating fabrics
1 yard Pellon fleece
⅝ yard lining fabric
Assorted lace trims and edgings, including enough to form a cuff around top of each stocking, if desired (see "Basic Terms and Techniques")
Embroidery materials (see "Embroidery Techniques and Stitches")
1 yard ribbon for hanging
Paper for patterns

Directions

Note: All measurements include ¼-inch seam allowances. When joining pieces, place right sides together and stitch ¼-inch seams. Press seam allowances to one side.

Patterns and cutting: Enlarge patterns given (see page 25). From each pattern, cut 2 of Pellon fleece; 2 of lining fabric, reversing one of each; 1 of backing fabric in reverse.

Patchwork layout: For each stocking, use 1 Pellon fleece shape as the foundation and, following the layout given on page 90, create a patchwork stocking front. Using lace and embroidery stitches, embellish layout as desired (see "Embroidery Techniques and Stitches").

Assembly: With right sides together and edges matching, join the top edges of the patchwork front to 1 lining section. Pin and baste a Pellon fleece shape to the wrong side of the backing; then join the top edges of the backing and the corresponding lining section. Open the front/lining and backing/lining pieces so they lie flat; leaving an opening along the back edge of lining for turning, join as shown (Figure 10). Grade seam allowances, clip or notch curves, and turn right side out. Slipstitch the opening closed. Push lining down into stocking, being sure that lining is wrinkle-free. Press upper edge of stocking lightly.

Finishing: For child's stocking cut a 10-inch length of ribbon; cut remainder in half for other stockings. Fold ribbon in half to form a loop, and sew ends securely to back of stocking near top of back seam. Add lace cuff by hand, if desired.

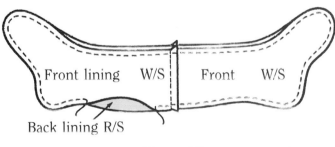

Front lining   W/S   Front   W/S

Back lining R/S

Figure 10

PATTERNS AND LAYOUTS FOR FAMILY CHRISTMAS STOCKINGS

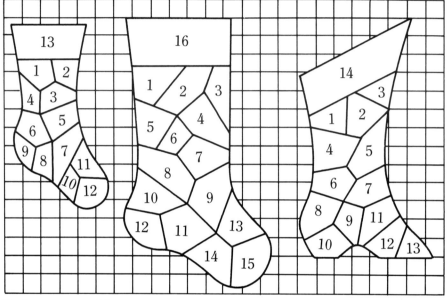

Each square = 1"

Tree Skirt

Size: 44 inches across

Materials

Note: All fabrics are 45 inches wide.

¾ yard master print
½ yard each of 8 to 10 coordinating fabrics
1¼ yards Pellon fleece
1¼ yards backing fabric
5 yards purchased corded welting, ¼ inch in diameter (or make your own
    with bias strips and cording)
Embroidery materials (see "Embroidery Techniques and Stitches")
Yardstick, pencil, chalk

Directions

Patchwork layout: Using Pellon fleece and master and coordinating fabrics, follow instructions for 44-inch-diameter circular layout (see Advanced Layout, pages 21–22) to create the tree skirt top. Using embroidery stitches, embellish entire layout as desired (see "Embroidery Techniques and Stitches"). Divide patchwork circle into eighths by folding in half vertically, horizontally, and diagonally; mark folds at edge with pins and mark center, then unfold with *wrong* (fleece) side up.

Shaping scallops: Following the diagram (Figure 11), mark each fold 1½ inches from edge. With chalk draw a smooth scallop between each pair of fold marks with the top of the scallop centered between the folds along the edge of the circle. With right sides together, place marked patchwork circle over backing fabric; pin together. Now cut along marked scallops through all layers. Before separating layers, mark position of slit: Using yardstick and pencil, connect the notch between 2 scallops with the center marking, as shown (Figure 12); draw a 6-inch-diameter circle at the center as well. Cut along marked line and circle, through all layers. Unpin and set backing aside.

Welting: Starting at outer end of slit, pin welting to right side of patchwork piece, matching edges of welting fabric to shaped edge of patchwork. Ease welting around curves and clip into fabric at notches as needed; end at other side of slit. (Do not pin welting along the slit itself; at each side of slit ease welting outward from scalloped edge so that cord will be caught in the seam-

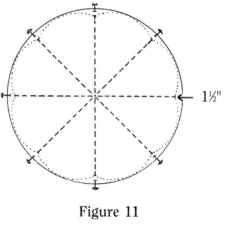

Figure 11

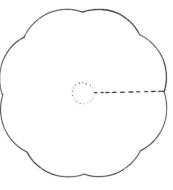

Figure 12

91

line at slit corner.) Using a zipper/cording foot, machine-baste all around, following the stitching on the welting fabric.

Finishing: With right sides together, pin backing to patchwork top, matching edges of slit, center circle, and scallops and enclosing welting. Leaving a 12-inch opening along one edge of slit for turning, using zipper/cording foot, stitch top and backing together all around, stitching over previous seam and taking a ¼-inch seam along slit. Reinforce circle at center by stitching again close to first stitching. Grade seam allowances, clip curves, trim slit corner, and turn right side out; press. Turn edge of opening under ¼ inch; pin to backing and slipstitch in place.

Christmas Bear

Follow instructions for bear under Patchwork Animals, pages 100–103, using print and solid fabrics and trims in Christmas colors; make bow in red.

Color Guide

The master print for the tree skirt is an abstract print in red, green, black and metallic gold. The other fabrics are solids—including some glazed chintz—and small prints, mostly in red, green, and black. The welting around the scalloped edge is black. Embellishment is kept simple and consists of embroidery stitches in traditional Christmas colors. For the bear, the fabrics are different but the basic Christmas color scheme remains the same. Touches of black lace trim and some bits of braid enhance the embroidery stitches.

Victorian
Baby Gifts

Ruffled Baby Quilt

Size: 32 × 48 inches, excluding ruffle

Materials

Note: All fabrics are 45 inches wide.
¾ yard master print
½ yard each of 8 to 10 coordinating fabrics, both prints and solids
1½ yards Pellon fleece
1½ yards backing fabric
Assorted trims, including a variety of lace and eyelet edgings and lace appliqués (see "Basic Terms and Techniques")
Embroidery materials (see "Embroidery Techniques and Stitches")
4½ yards pregathered eyelet edging, 1¾ inches wide

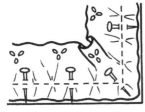

Figure 1

Directions

Note: All measurements include ¼-inch seam allowances. When joining pieces, place right sides together and stitch ¼-inch seams. Press seam allowances to one side.

Patchwork blocks (make 6): From Pellon fleece cut a 16½-inch square for each foundation. Follow the instructions for Basic Layout, pages 17–19, to create patchwork blocks for quilt top. Then, using trims, appliqués, and embroidery stitches, embellish the patchwork blocks as desired (see "Basic Terms and Techniques" and "Embroidery Techniques and Stitches").

Assembly: Join blocks in pairs to make 3 rows of 2 blocks each; then join rows to form a rectangle 2 blocks wide and 3 blocks long.

Ruffle: Cut pregathered eyelet edging to fit around the patchwork quilt top plus 1 inch. Join ends, making a French seam (see page 42). Press this French seam to one side. With right sides together and ruffle facing center, pin bound (or unfinished) edge of ruffle to patchwork quilt top, placing French seam at center of one side and easing ruffle around corners as shown (Figure 1). Machine-baste all around.

Finishing: From backing fabric cut a rectangle the same size as patchwork quilt top. With right sides together and raw edges matching (enclosing ruffle), pin top and backing together. Stitch around 4 corners and 3 sides, leaving an opening for turning. Grade seam allowances, trim corners, and turn right side out. Turn opening edges ¼ inch to wrong side; press. Pin, then slipstitch opening closed.

Color Guide

For the quilt, yellow and blue pastels are the main colors, repeated in several small floral prints and solids. Embroidery is also done in pastels, and the trims are white and off-white lace and eyelet bands and a few lace appliqués. The white ruffle is a pregathered eyelet edging. For the pillow, white substitutes for yellow; otherwise colors and embellishments are similar to those of the quilt.

Ruffled Baby Pillow

Size: 13 × 9 inches, excluding ruffle

Materials (enough for 2 pillows)

Note: All fabrics are 45 inches wide.
¼ yard master print
¼ yard each of 5 to 7 coordinating fabrics
½ yard Pellon fleece
Embroidery materials (see "Embroidery Techniques and Stitches")
Lace trim
1½ yards pregathered eyelet edging, 1¾ inches wide (for *one* pillow)
½ yard backing fabric
Polyester stuffing

Directions

Note: All measurements include ¼-inch seam allowances.

Patchwork layout: Cut a rectangle of Pellon fleece 13½ × 9½ inches for foundation. Follow instructions for Basic Layout, pages 17–19, to create a patchwork pillow top. Embellish with lace trim and embroidery (see "Basic Terms and Techniques" and "Embroidery Techniques and Stitches").

Ruffle: Follow instructions for ruffle of Ruffled Baby Quilt, page 96.

Finishing: Cut backing same size as pillow top, then follow instructions for finishing the Ruffled Baby Quilt, leaving an opening for turning and stuffing. Stuff pillow, then slipstitch opening closed.

Round Table Cover

Size: 44 inches in diameter

Materials

Note: All fabrics are 45 inches wide.

1 yard master print (includes enough for binding)

⅜ yard each of 6 or 7 coordinating fabrics

1¼ yards Pellon fleece

1¼ yards backing fabric

Assorted eyelet and lace trims and appliqués, ribbons, and seed beads (see "Basic Terms and Techniques")

Embroidery materials (see "Embroidery Techniques and Stitches")

Yardstick and pencil

Directions

Patchwork layout: Using Pellon fleece and master and coordinating fabrics, follow instructions for 44-inch-diameter circular layout (see Advanced Layout, pages 21–22) to create the table cover top. Reserve leftover master print for binding. Using trims, beads, and embroidery stitches, embellish entire layout as desired (see "Embroidery Techniques and Stitches").

Assembly: Cut backing same size as table cover top. With *wrong* sides together and edges matching, pin backing to top; machine-baste all around. Using reserved master print, cut and piece enough 1½-inch-wide bias strips (see page 29) to measure about 5 yards; prepare strip for binding. Open out one pressed edge of strip. With right sides together and edges matching, pin binding to table cover all around. Stitch in place, joining ends neatly (see page 27). Fold binding over edge to backing, pin in place, and slipstitch.

Color Guide

The master print for this table cover is a small white-and-aqua floral print on a pale lavender-gray background. The same fabric is used for the binding. Other fabrics are pale pastel prints and solids in mint green, lavender, aqua, and white. Assorted ribbons in matching colors and bands of white lace and eyelet, along with a few lace appliqués, are used to complement the pastel embroidery.

Patchwork Animals: Bear, Cat, Rabbit

Size: Approximately 20 inches high

Materials (for each animal)

Note: All fabrics are 45 inches wide.
¼ yard each of 6 or 7 different fabrics
1¼ yards Pellon fleece
Embroidery materials (see "Embroidery Techniques and Stitches" and individual instructions)
About 18 ounces polyester stuffing
Paper for patterns
Ruler, yardstick, pencil
Also:

For bear: Assorted lace trims
No. 3 pearl cotton for nose and mouth: black
Pair of safety eyes (buttons may be substituted, if not to be given to a small child)
1¼ yards each of satin ribbons in 2 different colors, one ⅝ inch and one ⅞ inch wide

For cat: ¼ yard fabric for bow
No. 8 pearl cotton for features: black, rose, blue, white

For rabbit: Assorted lace and eyelet trims
Pair of safety eyes (buttons may be substituted)
Pipe cleaners (optional)
No. 8 pearl cotton for features: pink
1 yard flat lace edging (or ribbon), 1¼ inches wide, for bow

Directions

Note: All animals are made the same, with exceptions given later. When joining sections, place right sides together and stitch ¼-inch seams, using tiny machine stitches for firmer seams. Where possible, press seam allowances to one side.

Patterns: Enlarge patterns given (see pages 25 and 105); *patterns do not include seam allowances.* Copy all markings onto patterns.

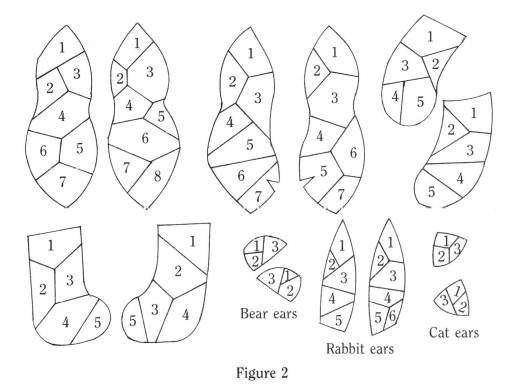

Bear ears

Rabbit ears

Cat ears

Figure 2

Cutting: *From Pellon fleece:* Cut pieces as follows, *adding ¼-inch seam allowances all around:* 2 each front and back; 4 each arm, leg, and ears. Transfer markings to 1 front section, then turn other front section over and transfer markings, so that you have 1 section as given and 1 in reverse. Repeat with remaining sections. The marked side of each Pellon fleece section is the *wrong* side.

Patchwork layout: See Basic Layout, pages 17–19, for technique. Then, following the layouts given here (Figure 2), use the Pellon fleece shapes as foundations and the fabrics to create the patchwork sections. Using trims for bear and rabbit only and embroidery stitches for all, embellish each section as desired (see "Embroidery Techniques and Stitches"). Mark eye positions on right side of front sections.

Assembly: Stitch darts on each back section. Then join sections, leaving openings for turning/stuffing, as shown (Figure 3). Clip inside curves and notch outside curves. Turn sections right side out. *For bear only:* Stuff ears lightly. *For rabbit only:* If desired, insert a pipe cleaner, bent in half, into each ear so that ears can be partially bent (not recommeneded if rabbit is for a small child).

With joined front section right side up, position and pin ears between markings; machine-baste in place, as shown (Figure 4). Pin and baste arms in place, as shown (Figure 4). At top of each leg, bring seams together at center as shown (Figure 4), then pin and baste in place (Figure 4).

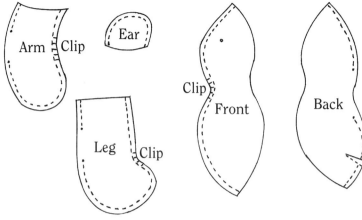

Figure 3

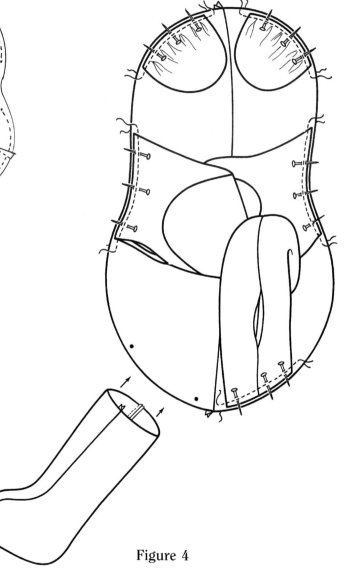

Figure 4

Now pin joined back section over front, enclosing ears, arms, and legs, as shown (Figure 5). Stitch all around, being careful not to catch free edges of enclosed sections. Grade seam allowances, clipping and notching curves. Turn right side out. If you are using safety eyes, attach them now. Stuff body very firmly, shaping head, tummy, and back as you go. Turn the edges of the back opening under and pin closed. Stuff arms and legs. Pin openings closed. Slip-stitch all openings.

Finishing: *For bear and rabbit:* Attach button eyes if you have not used safety eyes. ***For rabbit only:*** Shape upper part of face by sewing through head at base of eyes as shown (Figure 6); pull thread tight and fasten.

For embroidered features, follow diagrams given (Figure 7), as follows: ***Bear:*** black nose and mouth. ***Cat:*** eyes—black for outline and iris, blue for pupil; nose and tongue—rose; mouth—black; whiskers—white. ***Rabbit:*** pink nose and mouth.

Bows: *Bear:* Place narrow ribbon over wide ribbon, cut ends at an angle, and tie bow around neck. ***Cat:*** Cut bow fabric 6½ inches wide, across entire width. With right sides together, fold in half lengthwise. Then cut each end at an angle. Stitch along both ends and along long edge, leaving an opening for turning. Trim corners, turn right side out, and press. Slipstitch opening closed. Tie bow around neck. ***Rabbit:*** Notch ends of lace ribbon and tie bow around neck.

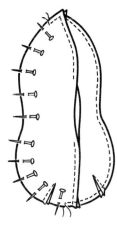

Figure 5

Figure 6

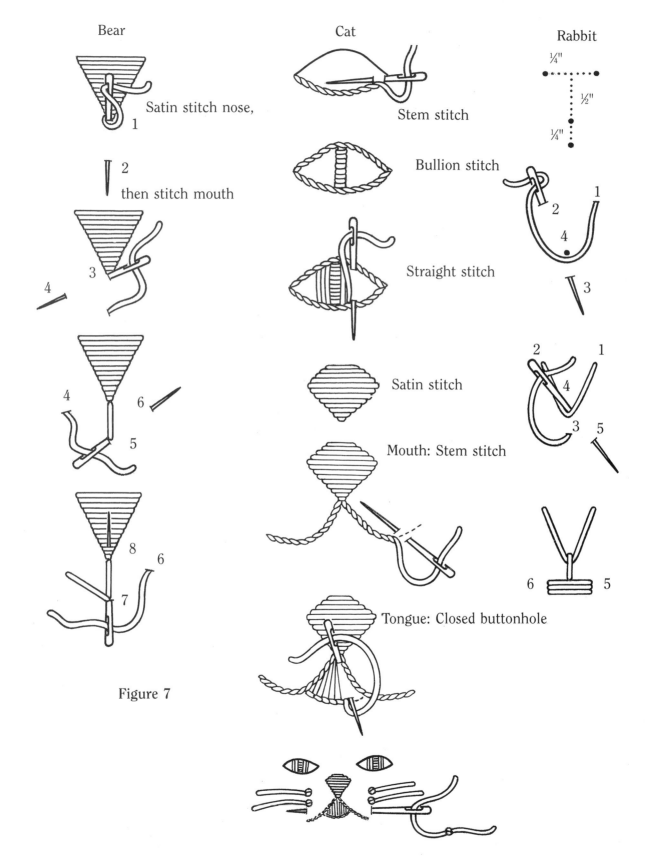

Bear

Satin stitch nose,

then stitch mouth

Figure 7

Cat

Stem stitch

Bullion stitch

Straight stitch

Satin stitch

Mouth: Stem stitch

Tongue: Closed buttonhole

Rabbit

¼"

½"

¼"

104

PATTERNS FOR PATCHWORK ANIMALS

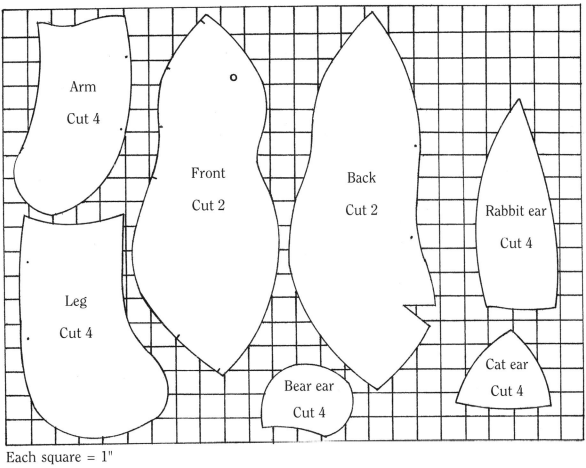

Arm
Cut 4

Front
Cut 2

Back
Cut 2

Rabbit ear
Cut 4

Leg
Cut 4

Bear ear
Cut 4

Cat ear
Cut 4

Each square = 1"

105

Three Little Kittens Quilt

Size: 58½ × 69 inches

Materials

Note: All fabrics are 45 inches wide.

2 yards master print in a light color (includes enough for sashing and border)

½ yard each of 10 to 12 coordinating fabrics

3¾ yards Pellon fleece

4 yards backing fabric

½ yard fabric for binding

Assorted lace trims and appliqués, eyelet, crocheted edgings, etc. (see "Basic Terms and Techniques")

Embroidery materials (see "Embroidery Techniques and Stitches")

6 baby mittens (purchase mittens or use commercial directions for knitting)

Paper for patterns

Ruler, yardstick, pencil

Directions

Note: All measurements include ¼-inch seam allowances. When joining pieces, place right sides together and stitch ¼-inch seams. Press seam allowances to one side.

Cutting: *From master print:* 2 strips each 4 × 62½ inches for side borders; 2 strips each 4 × 59 inches for top and bottom borders; 2 strips each 3 × 62½ inches for sashing (see page 26). Remainder of master print may be used for patchwork layout. *From Pellon fleece:* Border and sashing strips as for master print; 12 squares, each 16 × 16 inches, for patchwork block foundations.

Kitten patches (make 3): For each, place a piece of master print over a different kitten face embroidery pattern (see page 111) and trace the design onto the fabric. Embroider as indicated in appropriate colors, such as gray or yellow for fur, pink for nose and tongue, blue or green for eyes, etc.

Patchwork blocks (make 12): Using Pellon fleece square as foundation, follow the instructions for Basic Layout, pages 17–19, to create a patchwork block. Using trims and embroidery stitches, embellish each block as desired (see "Basic Terms and Techniques" and "Embroidery Techniques and Stitches"), incorporating a kitten patch into 3 of the blocks and adding a mitten to 6 other blocks.

Color Guide

The colors in this quilt are all pale pastels. The master print is a white-on-white print, to ensure visibility of the kitten faces, the nursery rhyme, and the pawprints. The binding is light blue, as is the embroidery on the sashing and border. The trims used to embellish the patchwork blocks are white and off-white, and the embroidery stitches are done in pastels to complement the fabrics.

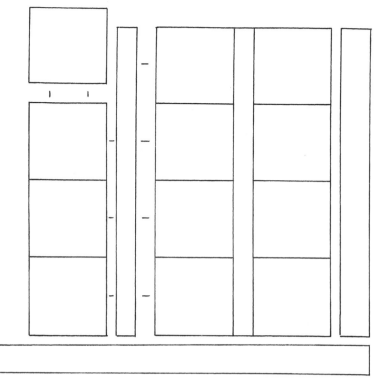

Figure 8

Assembly: Before assembling, place completed patchwork blocks on a flat surface as shown (Figure 8), adjusting them until you are satisfied with the arrangement. Then join 4 blocks to form a vertical row. Join 4 more blocks, then remaining blocks, to form 2 more vertical rows.

Sashing and border strips: Pin a fleece strip to the wrong side of each fabric sashing strip and each border strip; machine-baste a scant ¼ inch from edges all around.

Join 1 sashing strip to the right-hand edge of the first vertical row, then join the second vertical row, the other sashing strip, and the third vertical row, as shown (Figure 8). Join the side border strips, then the top and bottom border strips.

Backing: Cut backing fabric into two equal lengths. Then follow instructions on page 28 to piece the backing, assemble the quilt layers, and baste the layers together.

Quilting: Machine-quilt along vertical edges of sashing strips and around inner edge of border, directly over seamlines and through all layers.

Scallops: Trace and cut out scallop and corner templates (see pages 109 and 27–28). Using templates, mark rounded corners and scallops as shown (Figure 9). Stitch ¼ inch inside markings, through all layers. Trim excess ¼ inch outside stitching.

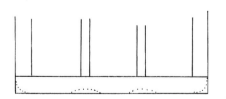

Figure 9

Binding: From binding fabric, cut and piece enough 1½-inch-wide bias strips (see page 29) to measure about 8¼ yards. Prepare binding as directed on page 29. Open out binding and, with right sides together and raw edges matching, beginning at center of one side, pin binding to quilt top; stretch binding along concave curve, ease along convex curves; stitch. Fold binding over edge and pin to back of quilt. Slipstitch in place, joining ends neatly (see page 26).

Finishing: Trace pawprint design and letters (see page 110). Transfer pawprints to sashing strips (see page 26), staggering them so that there are 10 prints on one strip and 11 on the other. Transfer letters to borders as needed to form the following rhyme excerpt:

    Three little kittens (*top*)
    Lost their mittens (*right side*)
    Don't know (*bottom*)
    Where to find them (*left side*)

Using No. 8 pearl cotton to match binding, work pawprint and rhyme designs in running stitch, through all layers.

TEMPLATES FOR THREE LITTLE KITTENS QUILT

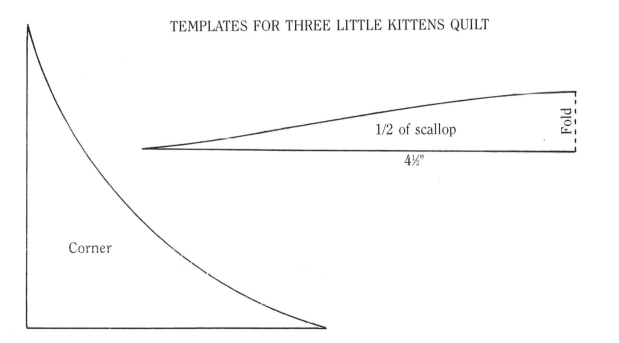

Corner

1/2 of scallop

4½"

Fold

Spectacular Quilts

Hydrangea Throw

Size: 51 × 68 inches

Materials

Note: All fabrics are 45 inches wide.

1½ yards master print

¼ to ½ yard each of at least 10 to 12 coordinating fabrics, including 4 or 5 solids

3 yards Pellon fleece

Assorted lace and trims (see "Basic Terms and Techniques")

Embroidery materials (see "Embroidery Techniques and Stitches")

3½ yards backing fabric (includes enough for binding)

Directions

Note: All measurements include ¼-inch seam allowances.

Patchwork blocks (make 12): From Pellon fleece, cut twelve 17½-inch squares for layout foundations. Then follow the instructions for Basic Layout, pages 17–19, to create 12 patchwork blocks. These blocks need not be identical, but they should be similar in number and size of patches and in the use of colors and prints.

Note: You may wish to vary one or two blocks by making a fan as part of the layout (see Special Layout Techniques, page 23). Embellish each patchwork block as desired, using laces, trims, and embroidery stitches (see "Basic Terms and Techniques" and "Embroidery Techniques and Stitches").

Assembly: Before joining blocks, lay them out on a flat surface, 4 across by 3 down as shown (Figure 1), shifting the blocks as needed until you are satis-

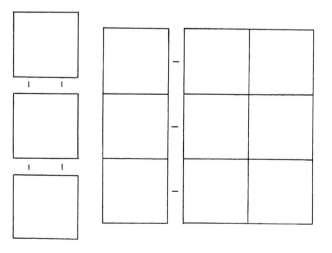

Figure 1

fied with the arrangement. With right sides together, pin and stitch the first vertical row of blocks together. Continue in this manner to join the remaining blocks into rows. Press the seam allowances open. Now join the rows; press the seam allowances open. The quilt top is now complete.

Finishing: From backing fabric, cut two 52-inch lengths across the entire width of the fabric; the remainder will be used for binding. Then follow instructions on page 28 to piece the backing (note that the seam will be parallel to the *short* edges of the quilt), assemble the quilt layers, and baste the layers together.

Starting at center and working out to edges, tie-quilt the layers together at 8-inch intervals, as shown (Figure 2), with *backing* side up and with single strand of pearl cotton in needle. Cut loops, divide strands in half, and tie knot securely against backing. Trim ends to ½ inch. Note that the thread should be nearly invisible on the patchwork top and the ends should be visible only on the backing side. Trim the backing to the same size as the top.

From remaining backing fabric, cut and piece enough 1½-inch-wide bias strips (see page 29) to measure about 7 yards. Prepare strip for binding as directed on page 29. Open out one pressed edge of binding. With right sides together and raw edges matching, pin binding to quilt top all around, mitering corners (see page 27); stitch, joining ends neatly (see page 27). Fold binding over the edge to the backing, pin edges in place, and slipstitch.

Figure 2

Color Guide

The Hydrangea Throw has a color scheme based on lavender and green, with accents of black and cream. Although the colors are somewhat subdued, the overall effect is quite exuberant, thanks to the number and variety of the fabrics used. The master print is a large, leafy floral print, and its colors of lavender, green, and cream are echoed in several other prints, all of them smaller in scale. Other prints have black or cream backgrounds; a stripe and several solids complete the picture. Embellishments include bands of lace and eyelet in different widths, lace appliqués, and a variety of embroidery stitches in various colors. For the backing and binding, a grayish blue moiré-print cotton was used. A coordinating pillow is made from prints and solids, predominantly grayed shades of blue, green, and lavender. The featured prints are floral, one with medium-sized, naturalistic flowers, the other with small, stylized flowers. To complement the embroidery, off-white lace trims and jumbo welting in dark blue are used.

Welted Pillow

Size: 16 × 16 inches

Materials (enough for 2 pillows)

Note: All fabrics are 45 inches wide.
¼ yard each of 2 different prints
¼ yard each of 4 or 5 coordinating solids
½ yard Pellon fleece
Assorted lace trims (see "Basic Terms and Techniques")
Embroidery materials (see "Embroidery Techniques and Stitches")
½ yard backing fabric
2 yards welting, about ½ inch in diameter (for *1* pillow)
16-inch-square pillow form or polyester stuffing

Directions

Note: All measurements include ¼-inch seam allowances.

Patchwork layout: Cut a 16½-inch square of Pellon fleece for layout foundation. Then follow the instructions for Basic Layout, pages 17–19, to create a patchwork piece for the pillow top. Then, using lace trims and embroidery stitches, embellish entire layout as desired (see "Basic Terms and Techniques" and "Embroidery Techniques and Stitches").

Welting: Cut welting into 4 equal lengths. Beginning at one corner, and with corded portion facing center, pin each length of welting to right side of patchwork pillow top along one edge, allowing ends to meet and extend at each corner, as shown (Figure 3). Using a zipper/cording foot, machine-baste welting in place, starting and ending the stitching just short of the corners, as shown (Figure 3).

Finishing: From backing fabric cut a square the same size as patchwork pillow top. With right sides together and edges matching, pin top and backing together. Still using zipper/cording foot, stitch around 4 corners (rounding them slightly and stitching across welting ends) and 3 sides, leaving an opening for turning and stuffing. Grade seam allowances, trim corners and excess cord, and turn right side out. Insert pillow form or stuff with polyester stuffing. Turn opening edges under and slipstitch opening closed.

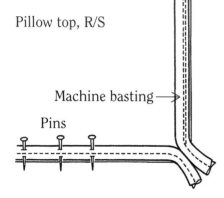

Pillow top, R/S

Machine basting →

Pins

Figure 3

Starry Starry Night Quilt

Size: Approximately 71 × 91 inches

Materials

Note: All fabrics are 45 inches wide.

2½ yards master print (includes enough for binding)

¾ yard each of 8 to 10 coordinating fabrics, including some solids

3½ yards black fabric for sashing and borders

5⅛ yards backing fabric

5½ yards Pellon fleece

Assorted lace and ribbons (see "Basic Terms and Techniques")

Embroidery materials (see "Embroidery Techniques and Stitches")

Paper for patterns

Directions

Note: All measurements include ¼-inch seam allowances. When assembling quilt, stitch all pieces with right sides together, taking ¼-inch seams. Press seam allowances to one side.

Cutting: Trace patterns A, B, C, and D (see page 121) for star blocks. *From black fabric cut:* 31 strips each 4½ × 17 inches for sashing; 14 strips each 2½ × 17 inches for borders; 80 from pattern B; 4 from C; 18 from D. Reserve any remaining black fabric for patchwork layout.

Select 2 or 3 contrasting prints and use these, along with some of the master print, to cut patches as follows: a total of 20 from pattern A; a total of 160 from B.

Note: Cut or mark off larger pieces (sashing, borders) first (see page 26), then cut patches.

Patchwork blocks (make 12): From Pellon fleece cut 12 squares, each 17 × 17 inches, for layout foundations. Set aside remaining fleece for later use. From master print, cut off ¾ yard and set aside for binding. Then, using remaining master print and coordinating fabrics, follow the instructions for Basic Layout, pages 17–19, to create 12 patchwork blocks. These blocks need not be identical, but they should be similar in number and size of patches and in the use of colors and prints.

Note: You may wish to vary one or two blocks by making a fan as part of the layout (see Special Layout Techniques, page 23). Using trims and embroidery stitches, embellish each block as desired (see "Basic Terms and Techniques" and "Embroidery Techniques and Stitches").

Star-center blocks (make 20): For each, use 1 print A and 4 black B. Join 1 B to each edge of A, as shown (Figure 4). From reserved Pellon fleece, cut a piece to fit the block; machine-baste to the wrong side of the block.

Sashing units (make 31): For each, use 1 black sashing strip and 4 print B. Trace and cut out corner template (see page 120). On right side, use template to mark and trim each corner of black strip as shown (Figure 5), then join a B, as shown (Figure 6). Back each unit with Pellon fleece, as for preceding blocks.

Assembly: Referring to Assembly Diagram (Figure 7), join sashing units to star-center blocks to form 5 sashing strips; join sashing units to patchwork blocks to form 4 rows of blocks, as shown (Figure 7). Then, keeping seams aligned, join sashing strips to blocks, as shown (Figure 7).

Border blocks (make 18): For each, use 1 black D and 2 print B. Join 1 B to each short edge of D, as shown (Figure 8).

Borders: For top border, join 1 end of a black border strip to the right-hand edge of 1 border block. Continue to add 3 border blocks and 2 border strips alternately, as shown. Make bottom border in same way.

For side borders, start with a black C, then join blocks and strips alternately in same way as for top and bottom borders, using a total of 5 blocks and 4 strips, and ending with another black C. Back each border with a matching piece of Pellon fleece.

Figure 4

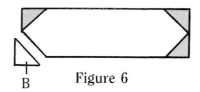

Corner of sashing unit

Figure 5

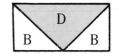

Figure 6

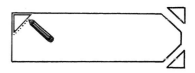

Figure 8

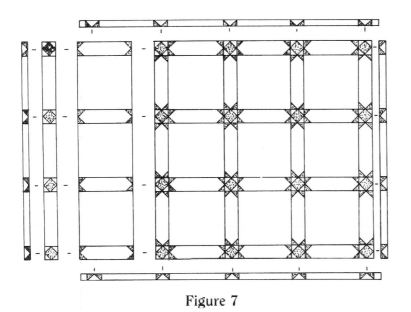

Figure 7

119

Keeping seams and points aligned, first join top and bottom borders to patchwork top, then join side borders. Quilt top is now complete.

Backing: Cut backing fabric into 2 equal lengths. Then follow instructions on page 28 to piece the backing, assemble the quilt layers, and baste the layers together.

Quilting: With quilt top right side up, machine-stitch around large patchwork blocks and around star-center blocks, directly over seamlines and through all layers. Trim edges of backing even with quilt top.

Binding: From reserved master print, cut and piece enough 1½-inch-wide bias strips (see page 29) to measure about 9¼ yards. Prepare strip for binding as directed on page 29. Open out binding and, with right sides together and raw edges matching, beginning at one corner, pin binding to quilt top, mitering corners (see page 27). Stitch all around, joining ends neatly (see page 27). Fold binding over edge to backing, pin in place, and slipstitch all around.

Color Guide

Black is the dominant color here, used for the sashing and borders as well as the traditional eight-pointed star motifs and some of the crazy-quilt patches. For contrast, fuchsia and turquoise prints (including the master print) appear in the star motifs as well as in the patchwork blocks, and muted dark blues and purples complete the picture. Trims are in the form of lace bands and edgings in various widths, all black, and narrow and wide ribbon. Embroidery is done in contrasting bright colors and metallics.

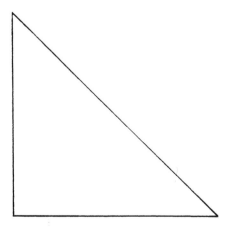

CORNER TEMPLATE FOR STARRY STARRY NIGHT QUILT

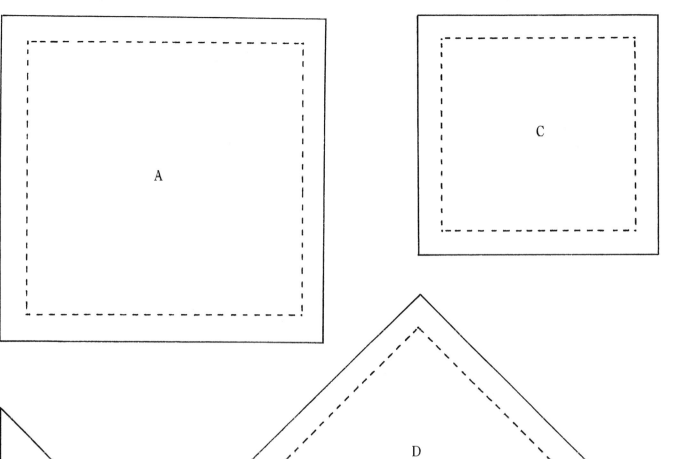

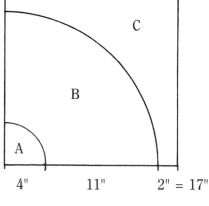

4"   11"   2" = 17"

Figure 9

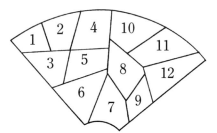

Figure 10

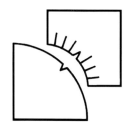

(a)

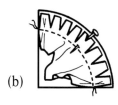

(b)

Figure 11

Victorian Fan Quilt

Size: approximately 82 × 82 inches.

Materials

Note: All fabrics are 45 inches wide.

6½ yards solid main fabric (for fan backgrounds, borders, sashing, and binding

4¾ yards backing fabric

½ yard each of assorted solid fabrics for patchwork fans (satin, velvet, crepe, taffeta, moiré, shantung, etc.)

6½ yards Pellon fleece

Embroidery materials (see "Embroidery Techniques and Stitches")

Assorted lace, ribbon, and trims (see "Basic Terms and Techniques")

Paper for patterns

Yardstick, pencil, string, compass

Directions

Note: All measurements include ¼-inch seam allowances.

Patterns: Using yardstick and pencil, on paper draw a 17-inch square. Using a compass and/or pencil and string (see page 22), draw curved lines and mark each section, as shown (Figure 9). Cut apart sections A, B, and C to use as patterns.

Cutting: *From main fabric and Pellon fleece:* Cut off a 2½-yard length each and set aside for borders and sashing. From remaining main fabric, use patterns A and C to cut 16 pieces each, *adding ¼-inch seam allowances to curved edges only.* ***From Pellon fleece:*** Use patterns A, B, and C to cut 16 pieces each, once again *adding ¼-inch seam allowances to curved edges only.* Borders and sashing, from both main fabric and Pellon fleece, and binding, from main fabric only, will be cut later.

Patchwork layout: For each fan, use 1 Pellon fleece B piece for layout foundation. Follow the layout diagram (Figure 10) to create a patchwork fan, varying fabrics and colors (and even the layout) so that no two fans are alike.

Fan blocks (make 16): Pin a main fabric A piece right side up to its corresponding Pellon fleece piece; stitch together ¼ inch from edges all around. Repeat with fabric and fleece pieces C. Mark centers of curved edges of A, C, and patchwork B. On curved edge of C, clip seam allowance as far as stitching; then, with right sides together and matching centers, pin C to B, spreading clipped edge of C to fit curved edge of B, as shown (Figures 11a, b); stitch. Clip curved edge of A in same way, then pin and stitch to other curved edge of B. Repeat these steps to complete remaining blocks.

Figure 12

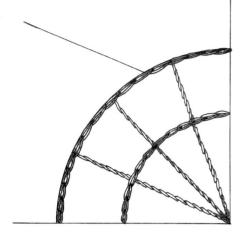

Figure 13

Fan embroidery (see pages 34–39): Using black pearl cotton, work a row of featherstitch along top of fan, just outside seamline (Figure 12). Then work a row of flystitch with chain anchor directly above first row (Figure 12). At base of fan, work spokes and arched radii, as shown (Figure 13). Edges of base and tassels will be added later.

Assembling the blocks: On reserved main fabric and Pellon fleece, mark 4 lengthwise strips, each 4½ inches wide, along the entire length; these will be used for borders. From remaining fabric and fleece cut 3¼-inch-wide sashing strips as follows: 3 strips each 74¾ inches long, and 12 strips each 17 inches long. Save remaining main fabric for bias strips. Pin and stitch each fabric strip to its corresponding fleece strip.

Refer to the Assembly Diagram (Figure 14) to position each fan block with sashing in between, as shown. With right sides together, stitch ¼-inch seams, and press all seam allowances toward sashing strips before crossing with another seam as follows: For first row, pin a short sashing strip to the right-hand edge of the first fan block as shown (Figure 14); stitch. Continue to add fan blocks and sashing strips until row is complete, then complete remaining rows in the same way. To set rows, pin and stitch 1 long sashing strip to the upper edge of Row 1, as shown (Figure 14). Continue in this manner to join rows of blocks and sashing strips until assembly is complete.

Figure 14

Figure 15

Borders: Cut previously marked strips of main fabric and Pellon fleece (see page 26); then cut each into the following lengths: 2 each 74¾ inches for top and bottom, and 2 each 82¾ inches for sides. Stitch each main fabric strip to its corresponding fleece strip. Join top and bottom borders to assembled patchwork piece (Figure 15); press seam allowances toward borders. Then join side borders (Figure 15).

Tassels: Complete embroidery of each fan by working chain stitch in black along straight outer edges of fan base. Make 2 black tassels (page 33) for each fan. Position on sashing or border as shown in photo, working black stem stitch "strings" between tassels and fan base (Figure 16). Work a loop of bullion stitch (page 39) at point of fan base.

Backing: Cut backing fabric into 2 equal lengths. Then follow instructions on page 28 to piece the backing, assemble the quilt layers, and baste the layers together.

Figure 16

125

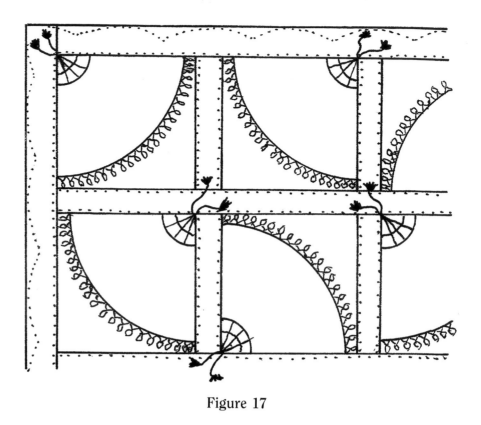

Figure 17

Quilting: With quilt top right side up, stitch along sashing and border seamlines, through all layers. Trim edges of backing even with quilt top.

Scallops: With quilt top facing up, mark one edge 4½ inches in from each end. Then divide the area between the marks into 7 equal sections (approximately 10½ inches each). Repeat along remaining edges. Using the pattern on page 127, make a paper template and trace curves along each edge between marks, as shown (Figure 17). Mark and connect corner curves, using part of template as needed. Stitch ¼ inch inside marked curves, through all layers; then trim on marked lines.

Binding: From remaining main fabric, cut and piece enough 1½-inch-wide bias strips (see page 29) to measure about 10½ yards. Prepare strip for binding as directed on page 29. Open out binding and, with right sides together and edges matching, beginning at one corner, pin binding to quilt top. Stitch, pivoting at notches between scallops. Fold binding over edge and pin to back of quilt, forming small pleats at notch of scallops. Slipstitch in place, joining ends neatly (see page 27).

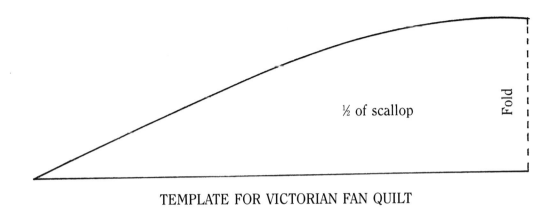

½ of scallop

Fold

TEMPLATE FOR VICTORIAN FAN QUILT

Garden Maze Quilt

Size: Approximately 84 × 104 inches

Materials

Note: All fabrics are 45 inches wide.

5½ yards muslin

3½ yards solid fabric for sashing and binding

¾ yard each of 8 to 10 fabrics for patchwork blocks, both solids and prints

7¼ yards Pellon fleece

6½ yards backing fabric

Assorted lace and eyelet trims and ribbons (see "Basic Terms and Techniques")

Embroidery materials (see "Embroidery Techniques and Stitches")

Paper for pattern

Ruler, yardstick, pencil

Directions

Note: All measurements include ¼-inch seam allowances. When joining pieces, place right sides together and stitch ¼-inch seams. Press seams to one side.

Pattern: To create pattern for triangle A, draw a 4-inch square on paper; cut out. Fold square in half diagonally and cut apart on the crease. Both halves may be used as pattern for triangle A.

Cutting: *From muslin cut:* Six 14-inch squares for floral blocks; 2 strips each 9 × 87 inches for side borders (see page 26); 2 strips each 9 × 84½ inches for top and bottom borders; 31 strips each 4 × 14 inches for sashing units; twenty 7-inch squares for sashing blocks; 72 triangles from pattern A. *From sashing/binding fabric cut:* 62 strips each 2 × 14 inches for sashing units; 20 strips each 2½ × 9¼ inches for sashing blocks; 36 strips each 2½ × 4 inches for sashing blocks. Reserve remaining fabric for binding. *From Pellon fleece cut:* Border strips same size as muslin, above; twelve 14-inch squares; twenty 7-inch squares; 31 strips each 7 × 14 inches.

Patchwork blocks (make 6): For each, use one 14-inch Pellon fleece square as a foundation. Follow the instructions for Basic Layout, pages 17–19, to create a patchwork block, using about 8 fabrics for each. Blocks need not be identical; you may vary them by using a different selection of fabrics for each.

Note: You may also vary one or two of the blocks by making a fan shape as part of the layout (see page 23). Embellish each block with trims and embroidery stitches as desired (see "Basic Terms and Techniques" and "Embroidery Techniques and Stitches").

Floral blocks (make 6): For each, use one 14-inch muslin square and one 14-inch Pellon fleece square. Using yardstick and pencil, lightly mark a 2-inch diagonal grid on the muslin square, as shown (Figure 18). Pin the fleece square to the back of the muslin square. Using No. 8 pearl cotton in desired color(s), work running stitch along marked grid, through both layers. Embroider flowers as desired (see pages 34–39) in the grid spaces marked with an asterisk (Figure 18). To finish the block, work a row of whipped running stitch (page 34) ¾ inch away from edges all around; then work a second row ½ inch inside first row, as shown (Figure 19).

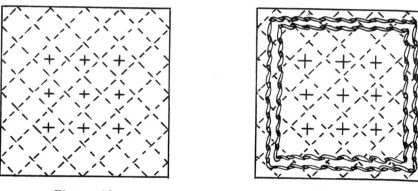

Figure 18   Figure 19

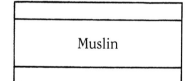

Muslin

Figure 20

Sashing units (make 31): For each, use one 4- × 14-inch muslin strip, two 2- × 14-inch fabric strips, and one 7- × 14-inch Pellon fleece strip. Join a narrow strip to each long edge of the muslin strip, as shown (Figure 20). Pin the fleece strip to the wrong side of the assembled piece and machine-baste close to edges all around. Embroider each sashing unit as shown (Figure 21), working a gentle S-curve in featherstitch, and a different floral motif in the center (see pages 34–39).

Figure 21

130

Sashing blocks (make 16): Step 1: Join a muslin triangle A to each long edge of a 2½- × 4-inch fabric strip, as shown (Figure 22); make a second piece in same way. Step 2: Lay a 2½- × 9¼-inch fabric strip diagonally across the center of a 7-inch muslin square, as shown (Figure 23); pin in place. Trim corners even with square, as shown (Figure 24). Step 3: Pin 1 piece made in Step 1 to the square as shown (Figure 25), matching its edges to the edge of the diagonal strip; stitch in place (sewing through fabric strip and muslin square) and unfold over muslin corner. Repeat with remaining piece from Step 1. Press block and trim corners as shown (Figure 26). Back each block with Pellon fleece. Use remaining pieces for corner sashing blocks.

Corner sashing blocks (make 4): Follow Steps 1, 2, and 3 earlier, with the following exceptions: In Step 1, make a total of 4 pieces. In Step 3, join only *1* piece from Step 1 to the diagonal strip. Press the opposite edge of the strip under ¼ inch; stitch in place close to pressed edge, as shown (Figure 27). Back each block with Pellon fleece.

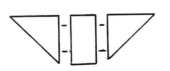

Figure 22

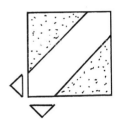

Figure 23

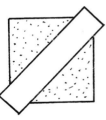

Figure 24

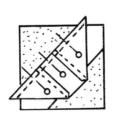

Figure 25

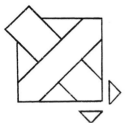

Figure 26

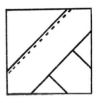

Figure 27

A = patchwork block   B = floral block

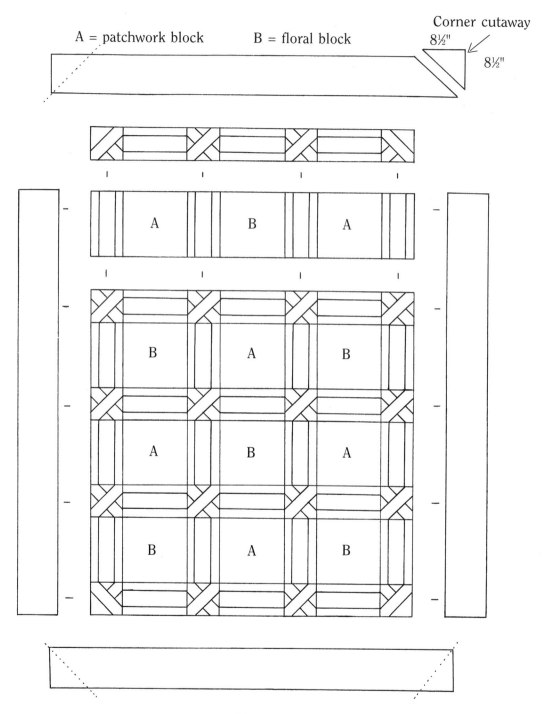

Corner cutaway
8½"
8½"

Figure 28

132

Setting the blocks: Referring to the Assembly Diagram (Figure 28), arrange the patchwork blocks, floral blocks, sashing units, and sashing blocks as shown. For the top row of sashing, join the upper-left-corner block to one end of a sashing unit; join a sashing block to the other end of the sashing unit. Continue in this manner, adding another sashing unit, another sashing block, and another sashing unit, then end with the upper-right-corner block. For the first row of blocks, join one long edge of a sashing unit to one edge of a patchwork block; join another sashing unit to the opposite edge of the patchwork block. Continue in this manner to add a floral block, another sashing unit, and another patchwork block, then end with a sashing unit. Assemble all rows in this manner, following the Assembly Diagram. When all rows have been assembled, join rows as shown in the diagram, starting at the top, and being careful to align the seams of the sashing strips.

Borders: Back each muslin border strip with a Pellon fleece strip. Join side borders first, then join top and bottom borders. To shape corners, mark each corner as shown (Figure 28), then cut along marked line, discarding the resulting triangle.

Quilt top is now complete.

Assembly: Cut backing fabric into 2 equal lengths, then follow the instructions on page 28 to piece the backing, assemble the quilt layers, and baste the layers together. Trim backing to same size as quilt top.

Quilting: Borders will have 4 rows of quilting; the innermost row, which need not be marked, is along the sashing/border seamline. Using yardstick and pencil, mark the outermost row 2 inches in from edge of quilt; mark 2 more rows evenly spaced between inner and outer rows. Quilting may be done by hand or by machine. Working from center outward, quilt around patchwork, floral, and sashing blocks and along all sashing seamlines, stitching directly over the seamlines through all layers. On the floral blocks, also quilt in a diamond shape formed by the 9 central squares of the grid. Finally, quilt the 4 rows around the borders.

Finishing: *Binding:* From reserved fabric cut and piece enough 1½-inch-wide bias strips (see page 29) to measure about 10½ yards. Prepare strip for binding (see page 29). Open out one pressed edge of strip. With right sides together and raw edges matching, pin binding to quilt top all around, mitering corners (see page 27). Stitch and join ends neatly (see page 27). Fold binding over edge onto backing, pin in place, and slipstitch.

Color Guide

For this large quilt, blocks of muslin and soft pastels (green, peach, yellow, and lavender) are tied together with sashing strips and binding in solid lavender. These colors are repeated in the abundant embroidery, which appears on both the patchwork blocks and the diamond-grid floral blocks, as well as the muslin of the sashing. The embroidery sampler wall hanging and pillow take their design and color cues from the quilt.

Embroidery Sampler Wall Hanging

- -

Size: Approximately 25 × 25 inches

Materials

Note: All fabrics are 45 inches wide.

½ yard muslin

1½ yards white-on-white print for outside border (includes enough for backing)

½ yard contrast solid for inside border and binding

1½ yards Pellon fleece

Embroidery materials (see "Embroidery Techniques and Stitches")

Yardstick and pencil

Paper for scallop template

Directions

Note: All measurements include ¼-inch seam allowances. Join pieces with right sides together (unless instructed otherwise), taking ¼-inch seams. Press seam allowances to one side.

Cutting: *From muslin and Pellon fleece:* Cut a 16-inch square of each. *From white-on-white fabric:* Cut white fabric crosswise into 2 equal halves; reserve one half for backing. From other half *and from Pellon fleece:* Cut outside border strips as follows: 2 each 5 × 17 inches for sides; 2 each 5 × 26 inches for top and bottom. *From contrast fabric:* Cut inside border strips as follows: 2 each 1 × 16 inches for sides; 2 each 1 × 17 inches for top and bottom. Reserve remainder for binding.

Sampler block: Mark center of muslin square by folding in half vertically, then horizontally. Using yardstick and pencil, lightly mark a 2-inch diagonal grid, having the center marking in the middle of a grid square, as shown (Figure 29). Pin the fleece square to the back of the muslin square. Using No. 8 pearl cotton in desired color(s), work running stitch along marked grid, through both layers. Embroider flowers or other designs as desired (see pages 34–39) in the grid spaces marked with an asterisk (Figure 29).

Borders: For the inside border, join side border strips to the side edges of the sampler block, then join top and bottom strips. For the outside border, pin, then machine-baste a matching Pellon fleece strip to the wrong side of each border strip. Join side border strips first, then join top and bottom strips; press seams onto inside border. Trim any excess to form a 25-inch square. Front of hanging is now complete.

Figure 29

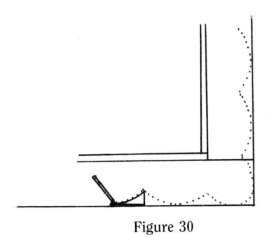

Figure 30

Finishing: Trim reserved backing fabric to same size as completed front. If desired, add a rod pocket for hanging (see page 27). With wrong sides together and edges matching, pin backing to front. *Scallops:* Using the pattern below, make a template and mark 3 complete scallops along each edge, as shown (Figure 30), then form corner scallops as shown (see page 28). Stitch ¼ inch inside marked curves, through all layers; then trim on marked lines. *Binding:* From reserved fabric cut and piece enough 1-inch-wide bias strips (see page 29) to measure about 3½ yards. Prepare strip for binding (see page 29).

Open out one pressed edge of strip. With right sides together, beginning at center of one side, pin binding to front of hanging. Stitch, pivoting at notches between scallops. Fold binding over edge onto backing, pin to back of hanging, forming small pleats at notch. Slipstitch in place, joining ends neatly (see page 26).

TEMPLATE FOR EMBROIDERY SAMPLER WALL HANGING

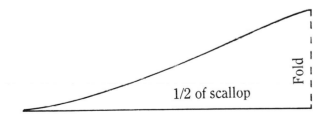

135

Tiny Sampler Pillow

Size: 9 × 9 inches, excluding edging

Materials

Two 9½-inch squares solid-color fabric
9½-inch square Pellon fleece
1¼ yards flat lace edging, ¾ inch wide
Embroidery materials (see "Embroidery Techniques and Stitches")
Ruler and pencil
Polyester stuffing

Directions

Note: All measurements include ¼-inch seam allowances.

Pillow top: Mark 1 fabric square with a 2-inch diagonal grid, as described for the Embroidery Sampler Wall Hanging, page 134, and as shown (Figure 31). Back the square with fleece as for the wall hanging, then embroider the grid and the asterisk-marked squares, using desired colors and designs (see wall hanging and "Embroidery Techniques and Stitches"). *Edging:* Join ends with a French seam (see page 42). With right sides together, pin lace edging to pillow top all around, with decorative edge facing center; ease trim around corners. Machine-baste close to outer edge.

Finishing: With right sides together, pin remaining fabric square to pillow top, enclosing lace edging. Stitch around 4 corners and 3 sides, leaving an opening for turning. Trim corners, grade seam allowances, and turn right side out. Stuff pillow, then slipstitch the opening closed.

Figure 31

Diamond in the Square Quilt

Size: Approximately 48 × 48 inches, excluding edging

Materials

Note: All fabrics are 45 inches wide.

1½ yards master print (includes enough for borders C and D)

¼ yard each of 7 or 8 coordinating fabrics

1¼ yards solid fabric for large triangles B and prairie point edging

3 yards Pellon fleece

3 yards backing fabric

Embroidery materials (see "Embroidery Techniques and Stitches").

Transparent gridded ruler and chalk

Directions

Note: All measurements include ¼-inch seam allowances. When cutting, always mark off longest and largest pieces first (see page 26); cut smaller pieces from remaining fabric.

Patchwork layout: From Pellon fleece cut a 28-inch square for foundation. Then follow the instructions for Intermediate Layout, page 20, to create patchwork piece A for the center of the quilt. Then embellish as desired with embroidery stitches (see "Basic Terms and Techniques" and "Embroidery Techniques and Stitches").

Large triangles: Cut two 20-inch squares from solid and two 20-inch squares from Pellon fleece. Cut each square in half diagonally to make 4 B triangles each of solid and fleece. With right side up pin 1 solid triangle to each fleece triangle; machine-baste all around a scant ¼ inch from edges. Join 1 B to each edge of A, as shown (Figure 32), to complete the diamond in the square. Press seam allowances toward B.

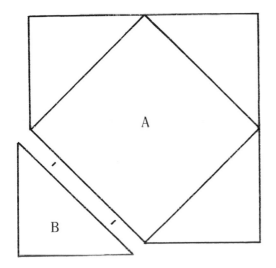

Figure 32

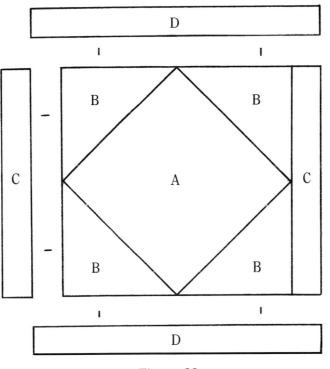

Figure 33

Borders: From master print and from Pellon fleece cut border strips length-wise as follows: **_Side borders_** (C): 2 each 5½ × 39½ inches; **_top and bottom borders_** (D): 2 each 5½ × 49½ inches. Layer, pin, and baste fabric and fleece strips as you did for B triangles. With right sides together, pin side borders C to opposite side edges of diamond in the square; stitch (Figure 33). Press seam allowances toward C. Repeat with top and bottom borders D.

Edging: From remaining solid, cut 88 squares each 2¾ × 2¾ inches. To make prairie points, fold each square in half diagonally (Figure 34a); press, then fold in half diagonally again (Figure 34b); press again. With raw edges matching and points facing center of quilt top, pin folded triangles to the right side of the quilt top, using 22 triangles for each edge and overlapping slightly as needed; position triangles at corners as shown (Figure 35). Machine-baste all around.

Backing: Cut backing fabric in half crosswise. Then follow the instructions on page 28 to piece the backing; keeping panels centered, trim backing to same size as quilt top. With right sides together, pin backing to quilt top all around; stitch all around, leaving about 15 inches open along one side for turning. Trim corners and grade seam allowances, then turn right side out. Press edges of opening to wrong side and slipstitch the opening closed. Press the edges and edging lightly.

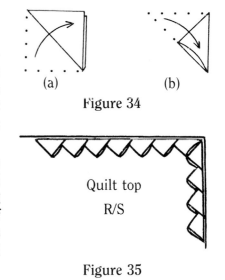

(a)   (b)

Figure 34

Quilt top
R/S

Figure 35

Finishing: With right side of quilt facing up, machine-stitch along the diagonal edges of the B triangles through all layers, directly on the seamline. Then stitch along the remaining edges of the B triangles in the same way. Using ruler and chalk, mark lines ¾ inch inside of and parallel to each outer edge of one B triangle. Working toward center, continue to mark parallel lines ¾ inch apart (Figure 36). Repeat for remaining B triangles. Using matching quilting thread, hand-quilt along marked lines.

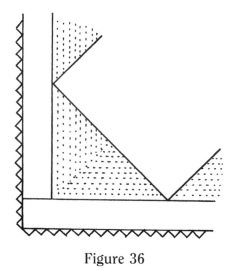

Figure 36

Color Guide

Our basic color scheme is blue and burnt orange. Master print and borders are a small-scale print on burnt orange background. Large triangles and edging are dark navy solid. Other fabrics making up the patchwork diamond are plaids in various shades of blue and burnt orange, 2 paisley prints, and medium blue and dark navy solids. Embroidery thread colors are shades of medium and light blue, and earth tones ranging from shades of rust to tan to beige.

Black Jewel Wall Hanging

Size: Approximately 43 × 43 inches

Materials

Note: All fabrics are 45 inches wide.

2¾ yards black cotton fabric (includes enough for borders, backing, and binding)

½ yard multicolor striped fabric

Small amounts of 6 to 8 coordinating dark solids and/or subtle prints

1¾ yards Pellon fleece

Embroidery materials (see "Embroidery Techniques and Stitches")

Ruler, yardstick, pencil

Directions

Note: All measurements include ¼-inch seam allowances.

Cutting: Cut off a 44-inch length of black fabric and set aside for backing; on remaining fabric mark off borders (see below and page 26) and bias strips for binding (see below). Remaining unmarked fabric may be used for patches. Cut off a 3½-inch-wide _crosswise_ strip (across full width of fabric) of striped fabric and set aside for middle border; use remainder for patches.

Patchwork layout: From Pellon fleece cut a 34-inch square for the layout foundation. Then follow the instructions for Intermediate Layout, page 20, to create the large center patchwork block. Using embroidery stitches along edges of patches and working flowers in center of several blocks, embellish the layout as desired (see "Embroidery Techniques and Stitches"). When block is completed, trim to 33½ inches square.

Borders: From black, cut border strips as follows: 4 each 44 × 4 inches for outer border; 4 each 44 × 1½ inches for inner border. Cut reserved striped fabric into 4 crosswise strips (across full width of fabric) each ⅞ inch wide for middle border.

From Pellon fleece, cut 4 crosswise strips each 5¾ inches wide.

To assemble borders, lay out 1 of each border strip as shown (Figure 37).

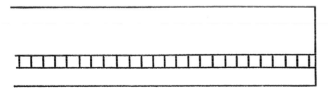

Outer border (black)

Middle border (stripe)

Inner border (black)

Figure 37

With right sides together, pin and stitch the strips together; press seam allowances open. Repeat with remaining strips, making a total of 4 sets of borders. Trim ends even so strips measure 43⅝ inches in length. Trim Pellon fleece strips to same size as border strips. Pin, then machine-baste a fleece strip to the wrong side of each border strip.

Join border strips and miter corners as for Victorian Teacup Quilt, page 57.

Note: This wall hanging is not quilted.

Finishing: Trim backing to same size as quilt top. If desired, add a rod pocket for hanging (see page 27). With *wrong* sides together and edges matching, pin backing to top; machine-baste all around. Using leftover black fabric, cut and piece enough 1½-inch-wide bias strips (see page 29) to measure about 5 yards. Prepare strip for binding (see page 29). Open out one pressed edge of strip. With right sides together and edges matching, pin binding to quilt top all around. Stitch, mitering corners, and join ends neatly (see page 27). Fold binding over edge onto backing, pin in place, and slipstitch.

Color Guide

The main color of this wall hanging is, of course, black. The jewel tones are introduced by a multicolored, striped glazed chintz, which appears in the form of patches as well as a narrow strip set into the wider black border. Other patches are made of the same black fabric that is used for the border and binding. The remaining patches consist of a variety of black or very dark fabrics such as taffeta, moiré, satin, brocade, and velvet. The patches are lavishly embroidered in strong colors, using both linear and filling stitches as well as floral motifs.

INDEX